PROMISES
OF THE
GOLDEN
PAIR

A WAY TO TEACH - A WAY TO LEARN

Authored by
Alexandra Marie Penn Ed.D.
From an idea by
Dennis W. Williams

Six Promises of the Golden Pair

SUMMARY

Six Promises of the Golden Pair outlines the advice offered to a new teacher who has begun the first term of school. Not only is this advice valuable to teachers, but it is essential guidance for anyone imparting knowledge and ideas to others.

This book is written in the form of a parable: it uses a simple, fantasy-like story that explains the meaning of the Golden Pair and the six principles that underlie teaching and learning.

As the story unfolds, the two characters—mentor and pupil—unravel the secret of the Golden Pair, an educational concept that posits teacher and student as equal components of a "golden" relationship.

In contrast to today's many complex educational theories, this short parable of time travel and platonic dialogue demonstrates how simple good teaching and learning can really be.

SIX PROMISES OF THE GOLDEN PAIR

"Golden Pair is an educational idea that looks at the teacher and the student as a pair and when the pieces of this idea fall into place, it is Golden."

Dennis Wendell Williams

goldenpair   **TM**

For Dennis, who lived and loved for the teachable moment—both as learner and teacher.

DEDICATION

<u>Six Promises of the Golden Pair</u> is dedicated to a man who really understood service above self and who was dedicated to improving education. He was a great teacher and avid learner; his greatest delight was watching a child experience the wonders of the world around her. He believed that reading was the key to lifelong learning and that everyone could learn. His life was a tribute to exploration and investigation and he died trying to learn more about the amazing planet he loved. This was my friend, my teacher and my late husband, Dennis W. Williams. May his memory be Eternal!

ACKNOWLEDGMENTS

To my children, Panos and Lora; thank you for your inspiration and encouragement over the twelve years it has taken me to complete <u>Six Promises of the Golden Pair</u>. This journey has been one of unexpected, sometimes painful stumbles but your lives and the memory of your father's have carried me to a humble beginning. For the publication of <u>Six Promises of the Golden Pair</u> is not the end of the story; it is a new beginning in the hearts and minds of readers who wish to carry on its simple message of great teaching and learning.

To my beautiful, life-long friend, Isabella; thank you for being my first editor and real writing teacher. Your editing prowess got me through English classes in high school and, even now, has added so much clarity to <u>Six Promises of the Golden Pair</u>. You were the only one I trusted to edit what was so near and dear to my heart.

To my wonderful spiritual protector and husband, Joseph; thank you for your prayers, emotional support and sincere objectivity. Your keen understanding of education, and especially instructional design, brought the book in my head to logical conclusions. Your unconditional love kept me looking forward at times when all I wanted to do was look back.

To the thousands of students who have been in my classrooms and schools over the past thirty-five years of my life, thank you for teaching me how to teach you!

Prologue

READING, WRITING, AND REMEMBERING

One of my most vivid childhood memories is of crawling into my parents' bed in the morning and pushing one of my Golden Books in front of my mother's face to read to me. Time after time, she would read the same words with the same wonderful expression in her voice and eyes. And I would look at the pictures as she turned the pages morning after morning. What I cannot remember is when I began reading those books back to her. I do not remember learning to read, just as I do not remember learning to walk or talk—I could just do it! Although memories of my early elementary education are spotty, I am certain I did not learn to read in school.

There were, however, other things I do recall about school. In kindergarten I remember cookies and milk, playing house, and missing my mom. I do not remember first grade much, aside from endless worksheets and a teacher who questioned the authorship of a poem I wrote about the days of the week. Second grade was only memorable because the teacher did not like me. She told my mother that I asked too many questions and that she should probably send me to a private school. When I was in third grade, my mother took on the New York City Public School System. She was convinced that my third-grade placement was not sufficiently challenging, so she insisted that I be tested. How this all came about and the details of the disagreement between my mother and the principal is a bit of a blur; but what is very clear to me is the recollection of sitting in the principal's office, taking a reading test and then learning that the results showed I was reading at the sixth-grade level. My mother's confidence in my ability convinced me that I could excel. Her belief in me was far more meaningful than my being "good" at school, passing tests, or finally going to private schools.

I often think about the other children in those classes at P.S. 71. I think about the promising children in kindergarten whose mothers did not send them to school already reading or ready to do so; the creative children in first grade who grew to resent school because of the repetitious busy work and their teachers' low expectations; the inquisitive children in second grade who stopped asking questions; and, finally, the smart children in third grade who grew discouraged because no one believed that they could learn.

Chapter I

TEACHING: IS THE JOB POSSIBLE?

"I never teach my pupils; I only attempt to provide the conditions in which they can learn."

Albert Einstein

In fifth grade, I wanted to be a scientist; in sixth, a doctor; by seventh grade, I had my hopes and dreams set on being a dancer. In high school, I acted and danced, painted and wrote. When I got to college, adolescent dreams competed with the many realities of making a living, so I pursued a collage of studies that included dance therapy, psychology, literature, special education, management, and more. This amalgamation of disciplines, a seemingly circuitous path to any career, paradoxically became what I now know to be the springboard for a lifetime of work in teaching and learning—a lifetime that began cruelly early one August morning, the first day of my teaching career, when 20 boisterous teenagers barreled through my classroom door.

I was not much older than my students, but I believed I knew exactly what and how to teach them. I had done my lesson plans and understood the content of my subject areas. I had observed other teachers' classroom management styles and even practiced them as a student teacher. It all seemed very doable. I was not going to be like one of those unsympathetic teachers with whom I had studied or whom I had shadowed. I would be caring, first; use the rules of instruction, second; and know my subject area, third. And yet, despite my good preparations and intentions, my introduction into teaching was not the sacred experience I had so naively envisioned.

The first day was a sickening blur and, at the end of, it I sat amidst piles of administrative debris, pages of faceless names, and volumes of irrelevant texts and lessons plans. That afternoon, as I watched my more senior colleagues lock up their tidy classrooms and rush off confidently to their orderly lives, I sat at my desk trying to figure out what had gone wrong. As I gazed out disconsolately over the empty desks, individual student faces began to merge into one, well-organized lesson plans seemed disjointed and meaningless, and I wondered whether classroom teaching was really possible. I had many more questions than answers as I looked back on the day, and unfortunately I had no "20/20 hindsight" that could help me prepare for tomorrow. I really did not know where to begin to do a better job. All the "teaching excuses" I had heard about and scoffed at became more real for me, and I wanted to indulge in them in order to feel better about myself. After all, I had done everything I was supposed to do.

```
TOP TEN TEACHING EXCUSES

  1.  Class size – too big
  2.  School Boards – too stupid
  3.  Principals – too rigid
  4.  Discipline – not enough
  5.  Text books – not on grade-level
  6.  Technology – not available
  7.  Parents – uninvolved
  8.  Counselors – uninformed
  9.  Teachers – untrained
 10.  Students – unprepared
```

How could it be my fault that, while I was passionate and sincere, my students seemed disinterested at best? Rarely would a student make eye-contact with me or volunteer an answer. There was a disconnection between what I believed I communicated and what the students did and said. In many ways, I'm not sure anything was understood. When I asked if there were any questions, I expected questions about information I had not provided. However, the questions I got were nearly always about subjects I had carefully explained or ones that were completely irrelevant. For example, to the question "Do you have any questions about your homework?" I was asked by one student, "What homework?" and by another, "Are we going to have free days?"

And then there were the eye-rollers and whisperers. These were mostly young women who waited for me to turn my back before leaning across the aisles to their friends with a snide comment, just loud enough for me to hear. The young men either retreated deep into their hoodies or overtly called attention to themselves by making inappropriate comments or actions.

The students who concerned me the most were those who sat with their arms crossed and their faces fixed in an "I dare you to make me do anything" expression. They seemed so shut down to anything I said or did; I had no idea how to reach them, how to penetrate their armor.

"Children today are tyrants. They contradict their parents, gobble their food, and tyrannize their teachers."

Socrates

"You can not teach a man anything. You can only help him discover it within himself."

Galileo Galilei

Sleep did not come easily that night and when the alarm clock finally sounded, I met the day with dread, knowing full well that I would face another round of doubt and frustration. As I opened my classroom door, the eternal optimist in me hoped that something in my plans or books or students would be suddenly different. I prayed for a miracle, one that would turn my classroom into the perfect teaching and learning environment.

Instead, what I found was an unfamiliar man sitting at the back of my room. His large frame was crammed behind a student desk, and yet he appeared perfectly at ease, the foot of one leg crossed comfortably over the knee of the other. He was reading a newspaper and chuckling, but he shifted his attention to me as soon as he heard the sound of the opening door and my startled gasp.

"Good morning. I've been waiting for you," he said, still amused by what he was reading. And as he looked up from his paper, I was taken by the whiteness of his hair and the strange iridescence of his eyes.

"What are you doing here?" I managed in as calm a voice as my pounding heart would allow.

"Reading today's paper and waiting for you," he replied. "I understand you need a little help with ... with what goes on here," and he looked around with the expression of a decorator contemplating an unkempt hovel.

My imagination invoked several scenarios to explain this interloper. First, he was some kind of sociopath meaning me harm; next, he was sent by the administration to uncover the degree of my incompetence before replacing me with someone who knew what he or she was doing. Either way, his presence did not bode well for my health, safety, or tenure.

"Who are you?" I insisted.

"You wanted a miracle. I am the best they could do," he replied calmly, as he folded his paper, uncrossed his legs, and freed himself from the confines of the student desk.

"Not funny," I pronounced sharply. "Did the administration send you? How did you know that... " I caught myself before revealing any more to this odd fellow who by now was walking toward me. I drew back.

"How did I know you wanted help?" he finished my sentence. "That's my job. Everyone is allotted a miracle worker, but they don't realize it until they accept the fact that they need one. Most people don't believe they need help, so they don't get it. The other part of my job is to sense when someone cares profoundly about a person or people and wants to make a positive impact. I know then that he or she is ready for a miracle, and I show up."

I knew I hadn't slept well the night before, but this was getting ridiculous. Certainly some much-needed coffee would make this fellow retreat back into the bad dream I was having.

"Miracle worker…?" I stumbled.

"And a pilot. I'll take you back to the fundamentals of learning and teaching—fundamentals you know but have forgotten. You will need these fundamentals if you are serious about making a difference."

I was reminded of yesterday's disaster. "Exactly when are you planning to do this? Over 100 students throughout the day will march in and out of that door starting at 7:10." I glanced at the clock, and it was nearly seven. "Just how far back can you take me in ten minutes, and what makes you think that that will help?"

"Oh, I'll need more than ten minutes," he laughed. "There are no magic bullets to your 'perfect teaching and learning environment,' and while you can wish for the power of a Vulcan 'mind-meld,' you'll have to ask yourself if that is really teaching."

"Mr. … I don't know who you are or where you came from, but my day is about to start with or without your help. So, if you don't mind, there are a few last-minute things I need to do before my first class begins." In response, the stranger walked past me toward the still-open door.

"Let me know when you'd like to begin," he offered, looking over his shoulder. And as he did so, the first rays of sun crept through the window, lighting the strangely iridescent irises of his eyes.

"Begin what?" I called back.

"The Six Promises, of course."

"What six promises?"

"The Six Promises of the Golden Pair," he replied and was gone. I took a deep breath. Stress could powerfully alter a person's ability to function rationally, but could it make you delusional? I was relieved he was gone but, at the same time, had a strange yearning for what he seemed to offer.

Day two was worse than the first. The students could sense my insecurities, and I could see that any confidence they had in me would soon wane. I was going to have to do something fast if I hoped to keep my job and hold on to my dream of inspiring young minds. I wondered if all new teachers went through this struggle. Was I particularly inept, or did the others just not care enough to worry about being effective? Maybe the stranger had been right: I did need help. I certainly cared deeply about making a difference in the lives of my students.

ALL CHILDREN CAN LEARN

"The art of teaching is the art of assisting discovery."

Mark Van Doren

As the last group of students jettisoned out of my classroom, Mr. Pilot's larger-than-life frame filled the doorway. Backlit by the afternoon sun, the mysterious figure was actually a welcome sight.

"You look like you are ready to go." he pronounced.

I seemed to recall that he had mentioned some sort of "promising" exercise, but there had never been any mention of "going" anywhere. Why would I go anywhere with this man whose motives were questionable and whose name I did not know?

"Barnabas, my name is Barnabas. Mentor and pilot at your service—to help you fulfill your desire for an excellent learning and teaching environment. My motives are simple. Pure and simple."

He was reading my thoughts again, and this made me very uncomfortable. But I was desperate, and desperate people do desperate things. I must be out of my mind, I thought.

"Where are we going?" I asked, as I packed up my work to take home.

Barnabas, who had been folding his newspaper, ignored my question. "I do like to keep up with what goes on here—so much going on. What I really like is the comics section. I learn a lot from cartoons."

"From comics…?"

"Yes, comics can cut to the quick of most issues. They are whimsical reflections of our times and are often more efficient than other types of media. Take this one here, for example…"

"Maybe this is a bad idea…" I mumbled, silently questioning the man's discernment.

"No, really, you should try reading them." And Barnabas opened the paper to a Calvin and Hobbs Cartoon.

I'll leave this for you. Let me know what you think." And with that he rose and started for the door.

"This IS a bad idea" I repeated under my breath but started following him, nevertheless. "Wait. You still haven't told me where we are going."

"To the place where you first learned that all children can learn. Do you remember?"

I caught up with him, "No, what place?"

"I'll show you."

Trying to keep up with his giant strides, I recalled my first teaching experience and then, amidst a flood of memories, muttered, "Yes … but how can we go there now?"

"All things are possible. Don't worry. I'll have you back before dark."

We climbed into an old, open-style jeep that was parked in back of the school and then drove to a private airport less than a mile away. I didn't remember ever having seen that little airport with its tiny building, which looked more like a storage shed than an airport terminal. The runway was small—just long enough for modest, private aircraft—and resembled no airport I had ever seen. By the look of it, there were no jets coming or going from this unkempt airstrip on which there was a sole, tiny plane that looked like something left over from WWII. Certainly we could not be flying in that, I thought.

"That's 'er", Barnabas answered my thoughts. "That's the T-50 Bobcat. She's a Cessna beauty, don't you think? Built in 1943, but doesn't look a day over 50."

"I'm not sure about this," I protested, trying to calm my heart, which was pounding so loudly I feared he could hear it.

Barnabas turned to look at me and, for the first time, smiled back with a very genuine, "it's going to be all right" expression. The iridescence of his eyes seemed less strange than when I had first met him—warmer and more inviting. His entire demeanor was so disarming and reassuring, that I became lost in his almost hypnotic aura.

Once we were airborne, my mind rushed ahead of the flight to my very first experience working with children with disabilities. It was a voluntary job at a school for students with visual impairments and other sensory or cognitive disabilities. It was during a time when I was exploring avenues for graduate work—the period before I started my Masters Degree in Special Education. I remembered how nervous I was before my first day as a volunteer teacher's assistant. As I rode my bicycle through the busy streets of Manhattan toward the school, I nearly turned back several times. But by the end of that first day, I was in love and felt called to teach—particularly students with disabilities— but that seemed like a lifetime of academia ago.

Barnabas broke my reverie and reminded me of our mission: to revisit the fundamentals of teaching and learning. "When we get to the school," he said, "don't be surprised when you see yourself as you were when you were last there. You will have a chance to watch yourself, together with the other teachers and the students, in a rerun of the time you first realized that all children can learn."

This flying thing was already strange, but time travel? What next?

The ground came up to meet our little plane, but there was no runway beneath us—no airport or even space to land. The city got frighteningly closer and closer until magically, and before I knew it, we were transported to the familiar halls of the school that had more to do with my wanting to become a teacher than any other aspect of my life. It was the place where I had learned to care deeply about making a difference in the life of a child. Barnabas was right; it was like watching a rerun of life, and the main character was me.

As he led me into a classroom I had not seen for years, Barnabas asked, "What do you remember about this classroom?"

The room was bright and bubbled with movement. My senses were awash with the mixture of music, puzzle-pieces, and play-dough. Smells of freshly baked cookies hung in the air, sweetening the already delightful picture of happily engaged children whose shining faces reflected the pleasures their eyes could not see. Touch, smell, and hearing were the senses through which these children, who were blind, learned. I remembered how amazed I had been at the wealth of teaching tools designed to accommodate the ways in which these students learned best.

"This was where I first understood that not everyone learned in the same way, that you had to be willing to try anything to get your students to achieve, and that success could be measured in the smallest of increments," I replied.

Although it felt a bit bizarre at first, I watched myself seated at a low, child-size table across from a young girl not more than five years old. I was working with her on the concepts of forward, backward, left, and right. Her bright, red dress and large, white hair bow contrasted sharply with her quiet curiosity. A younger version of me helped her to carve lines into soft clay. I guided her little hands—hands that would soon learn to read Braille—reinforcing the four directions in relation to her position in space.

"Barnabas, look at how surprised and delighted I was at her successes," I cried as she performed the simple directions independently, improving with each try. "This is what helped me understand that all children can learn. I'd forgotten that. I'd forgotten that very basic concept. If there is a promise to be learned here, I think I know what it is." Barnabas waited as I formulated the promise in my mind.

"I promise to teach you," I finally declared.

"Yes, that's right," he smiled. "So where did you learn those skills?" he asked and pointed to the young volunteer who was me, reinforcing correct responses to my directional commands.

"I'm not sure, but I guess I used my past experiences and knowledge. I also had a strong desire to do anything it took to teach the concepts. I cared deeply because a lot was riding on the students' understanding of those directional concepts."

"Go on…"

"If my students, who were blind, had not learned their directional concepts, acquiring other skills, such as how to get around and reading and writing, would have been next to impossible."

"Looks to me like you were pretty successful at getting your students to get around independently and, in some cases, to read Braille," he remarked as we looked on. "And I don't see any evidence of the use of a Vulcan 'mind meld' either, if I may add."

"How do you know that?" I teased.

"Because you just said that your students needed to be able to build on the directional concepts they learned by applying them to more complex tasks. Mind melds would not allow them to do that because *part of learning is learning.*"

"I don't understand. What do you mean by 'part of learning is learning'?"

"You just said it yourself: the teaching and learning that took place here was incremental, building from the simple to the complex. That is how all good teaching and learning happens. You've always understood that. You've just forgotten how to practice it."

"You mean, just as in some cases we had to teach the simplest, most fundamental concept before going on to the next?" I asked.

Barnabas nodded. "Yup. Well, if we are to get home before dark, we must leave now." He walked out of the classroom towards the corridor.

"Wait, Barnabas, there is another reason the students achieved."

"Oh, and what was that?" he questioned knowingly.

"The teachers and students taught me to … well … we really cared … cared deeply about these kids." Soft squeals and chatter filtered through the open classroom door to where we stood.

"You mean there was a lot of love going on?"

"Yes, I guess you could say that. I had forgotten that, too. That's what kept me coming back here every day as a volunteer. That's what made me want to teach. I just haven't been…"

"Practicing it much?"

"I guess not," I confessed and, lost in thought, followed Barnabas down the hallway to an elevator.

"We'll take this one," he said pushing the up button on the wall. The elevator doors opened immediately. We no sooner stepped inside than the entire elevator transformed itself into the little airborne Cessna cockpit.

"Whew, how do you do that?" I exclaimed, bracing myself for the journey and reaching for a seatbelt.

"I will take that as a rhetorical question," he winked and flew us back to the present—and that strange little airport. It was a quick jeep ride to the school where Barnabas parked next to my vehicle and helped me transfer my books and papers.

"Thanks," I said, still a bit dazed from the afternoon's adventures.

"Oh, no problem. All in a day's work," he shrugged.

"No, I mean the lesson. Thank you for the lesson."

"So what did you learn?"

"That the job IS possible and *ALL children can learn*."

"And the promise…?"

"*I promise to teach all students what they need to know now so that they can apply it to future learning.* No more wishes for Vulcan 'mind melds' or magic bullets because learning is part of learning."

"Excellent! That was the first part of your test."

"What do you mean, first part?" I shot back.

"The real test is whether or not you can apply the principle you have just remembered and keep the First Promise. Tomorrow, you will decide for yourself if learning has taken place—both for you and for your students. Remember what you learned and apply it," he said as he got into his jeep.

"Oh, and don't forget the most important thing of all," he added while revving the engine. "Keep working on love." I watched the small vehicle disappear into the strangely lit dusk. Purple- and rose-colored clouds papered the sky from which we had just landed, and I stood in the empty parking lot struggling to accept the reality of what had just happened.

Barnabas was right: the First Principle and the First Promise were fundamental. They were what I had learned and offered to my "students" while still a student myself. When had they dropped off my radar screen?

When I got home that evening and started to review my lessons for the next day, I stopped and looked more carefully at the list of names on the roster for the class I was preparing. It took a little while, but I strained to really see the faces of those students. I then took out the writing samples they had done on the first day. As I looked at the names, remembered the faces, and read the students' work, I tried to do as Barnabas had asked: apply the First Principle, "*All children can learn,*" and fulfill the First Promise, "*I promise to teach you.*"

"I promise to teach you, I promise to teach you," I repeated to myself as I worked. And then I added, "I will teach you at the level you are, not where I want you to be; and I will teach you what you need to know, understand and be able to do to get to the next level of where you need to be. You and I will set the achievement bar realistically high and we will celebrate every increment of improvement, no matter how small, as you achieve your learning goals." I changed my lesson plans that evening, aligning them with my renewed vow to *teach ALL students, no matter their learning style, level, or need.* And in my planner, I circled Principle One: *All children can learn!*

What a difference a day can make. My journey to school on day three was filled with anticipation: I could hardly wait to apply what I had learned. I also hoped I would find Barnabas waiting for me as he had the day before. I opened my classroom door and looked around anxiously, but he was not there. I was disappointed I could not share what I learned last night, but then remembered what he had said about the rest of the test: I needed to apply what I had learned. So, as the clock closed on 7:10, I glanced at the cartoon Barnabas had left open on my desk, the only evidence that he had really been there:

I readied myself to make good on the First Promise.

As the students trickled in and took their seats, they noticed the statement I had written on the whiteboard.

Promise # 1: I promise to teach YOU

The "you" was boldly displayed in all caps. It was crucial that the students realize that the YOU was not the class or even a small group within it; it was not the students in my other classes; it was the individual YOU. The time I had taken the night before to get "to know them" from their writing samples was time well spent. As I passed back the papers, the students read the personal notes and questions I had written to them. These were not just the dispassionate editorial marks and squiggles I might have written before my consciousness-raising adventure with Barnabas. My comments indicated I wanted to get to know my students. I wanted to learn details about their lives; I wanted to understand their strengths and weaknesses, their likes and dislikes. Finally, I needed a sense of what they wanted to do with what they learned.

Their class assignment was to respond in writing to my queries—an invitation to tell me about themselves by responding to targeted questions. It was the infant beginnings of what would become a rich and informative dialogue between learner and teacher.

I repeated the activity with each new class, and by the time the last set of students entered my room, they were already privy to the drill. It seemed that word had got round about my Promise and about the "different" approach my students and I would take to teaching and learning. I knew I was doing something right when a few of my students lingered in my room after dismissal to show their friends what I had written to them. A few of them even stopped to talk to me about my comments and to qualify what they had written in response to my questions. They liked the conversation and saw the first glimmers of someone who cared, someone who was practicing love.

I was pleased with the way the day had gone, but could not stop wondering what I could do to make it better. When would I learn the other Five Promises and, come to think of it, what was the Golden Pair? Barnabas had mentioned that concept on the first day and had not returned to it since.

"Well done, New Teacher! You passed the second part of the test!" Barnabas bellowed, as he seemed to materialize from nowhere.

"You startled me!" I jumped.

"Inappropriate stress response," he retorted, as he strode over to a student desk and squeezed himself into the tightly fitting seat. "I promise to teach YOU," he read out loud. "That's good, very good! So, tell me about your day."

I rambled on about the previous night's alterations of lesson plans—my new approach to addressing individual student learning styles and levels and what they needed to know, understand, and be able to do. I shared what I believed to be the awesome results of the day's teaching. My enthusiasm was obvious as I moved about the room, reenacting the day's events. When I finally stopped to take a breath, I noticed Barnabas smiling from ear to ear, like a proud papa.

"I'm not surprised!" he declared, shaking his head. "No, not surprised at all. But I do have one question for you."

"What is it?" I asked.

"How do you know that you fulfilled the First Promise to EACH of your students?" His question gave me pause, and I was not sure how to answer. "It sounds like you achieved your teaching objectives, but did your students achieve their learning objectives?"

"I don't know," I answered honestly and must have looked like a deer in the headlights.

"Looks to me like it's time to discover the Second Promise. You'll need this," he said, as he threw me an old flight cap and started for the door.

"By the way," he called back. "I'm glad you appreciated the Calvin and Hobbs cartoon. See what I mean about efficient media? It really grabs you. Don't you think?"

goldenpair

Chapter 2

WHAT ARE TEACHING AND LEARNING?

"When one teaches, two learn."

Robert Half

But why the flight cap? I wondered as I fingered the fraying head gear. Our last flight was in a small but sturdy Cessna; this looked like something barnstormers wore in the 1920s. I noticed that Barnabas held another cap, which looked a size or two bigger than the one he had tossed me.

"What's this for?" I asked.

"You'll see," he replied.

Once at the airport, I understood: parked in the middle of the small runway was an open cockpit biplane.

"No way! Where's the other plane—the one we took yesterday?"

"One of my colleagues needed it. She and her student were going much farther than we will. This is a great little gal, a 1943 WWII Stearman Bi-Plane. I thought you'd enjoy the adventure. The day is picture perfect for some open cockpit flying." He looked up and around at the cloudless blue sky. "You do remember how much you enjoy adventures, don't you?"

"What do you mean?" I could sense this leading to another of Barnabas' "teachable moments." How did he know so much about me?

"When was the last time you acted on the risk-taker side of you?"

It was hard to think through the pounding in my chest and the shortness of breath I was experiencing.

"It was probably when I learned to scuba dive. Yes, that was the last time. It was in the Bahamas and..." I thought back to that experience and shuddered. "Why do you ask? What does scuba diving have to do with flying around in this ... this open cardboard box with wings?"

"Why did you want to learn to dive?"

More questions! I was already stressed and did not need or want the third degree. Thinking about my scuba experiences was simply heightening my anxiety about the impending flight.

"I don't know... I guess it was because ... well, because it would be an adventure.

"And so will this be 'an adventure.'"

"An adventure, okay, okay," I concentrated on slowing down my breathing. A light breeze calmed my clammy skin and heart rate. "But what do adventures have to do with the next promise? Does it have anything to do with teaching versus learning objectives?"

"Exploration."

"Exploration?"

"Yes, and the fact that teaching and learning are not spectator sports."

TEACHING AND LEARNING ARE NOT SPECTATOR SPORTS

"The teacher is no longer merely the-one-who-teaches, but one who is himself taught in dialogue with the students, who in turn while being taught also teach."

Paulo Freire

Adventure, exploration, spectator sport—Barnabas had really piqued my curiosity by then and also challenged my ego. I thought of how unadventurous—almost sedentary—I had become over the past several years as I focused on school and teaching. Teaching and adventure: what could those two possibly have in common, except the potential for an oxymoron? And before I knew it, I was donning my flight cap, climbing into a heavy jacket and securing my harness as I hunkered down into the rear tandem passenger seat of the tiny biplane. Barnabas had already climbed into the cockpit directly in front of me and was preparing for the flight. With ritual-like routine he performed a series of checks and tests on the craft, talking to himself as he would to a co-pilot. His large frame filled the front seat so I focused on his shoulders, which gave me a strange—perhaps false—sense of safety.

"Where are we going, anyway?" I asked and focused on remaining at ease.

"To the Bahamas, of course," he shot back.

"What!" I shouted as the plane taxied down the runway. "Not in this!" But it was too late for, before I knew it, we were circling over the airport toward our flight path. I quickly pulled the flight cap over my ears and fastened the strap tightly under my chin. When I reached for the seatbelt, I noticed that I was mysteriously, not only belted, but harnessed. The little biplane and I were one.

I watched as the ground grew less and less visible and the clouds grew more and more dense, surrounding us like massive pieces of cotton candy. The sensation of the wind in my face and the view of Barnabas' back, with his white hair blowing wildly, took my mind off the fact that we were flying single engine over the ocean. Or were we? Our arrival in the Bahamas was as unorthodox as it had been in New York City. This time, however, Barnabas circled the plane down until we were both inexplicably transported to where I already saw myself shivering in the deep end of the training pool where my unsettling scuba adventures had begun.

Barnabas and I stood gazing over the side of the pool as a small group of scuba divers hovered together in a circle at the bottom of the deep end. They were learning how to remove and reinsert their regulators from their mouths, a scuba skill practiced in case the breathing piece is accidentally knocked out of a diver's mouth. The tricky thing about that skill is that you have to remember to "purge" the device from water before putting it back into your mouth and breathing. Should you forget to purge, you would have the unforgettable experience of breathing in a regulator full of water—a very unpleasant and dangerous mistake. As the divers practiced, their tiny bubbles rose vertically, surfacing in huge, halo-like circles above them. From where we stood, it was difficult to see which one was me. However, I was able to pick out the instructor easily. He was the one with the long, blond hair flowing in the aqua-blue water—flowing as nebulously as his instruction, I recalled.

"Do you remember this?" Barnabas asked.

"How can I forget it? I nearly killed myself!" Having said that, I watched as one of the divers shot up to the surface of the water, ripping off the mask and breaking through the halo of bubbles with gut-wrenching gasps.

"That's me," I whispered and I turned away from the sounds of my own desperate attempts to get air into my water-filled air pipes. "Why are we here?" I questioned, desperate to move away from the scene.

"Why did that happen?" he probed.

As I looked back to answer, I saw the pool water glisten in the iridescence of his eyes; I saw myself there too as I was on that day: shivering, embarrassed and tearing off my scuba equipment. I had been so traumatized that I nearly dropped out of the course. It was fortunate that nothing more serious happened to me after I breathed in without purging my regulator and breaking the cardinal scuba rule: "Never ascend while holding your breath."

"But why did that happen?" he repeated. "What went wrong?"

"I'm not sure. I want to say I was careless. But, at the same time, I'm not sure I was prepared. I didn't understand all the rules."

"Did the instructor explain what could happen? Did you read the instructional materials?"

"Yes, but I didn't get it. I mean, I thought I got it while sitting in the safety of the classroom with the teacher going through his canned lessons, which he delivered perfectly in a voice that seemed like the voice-over to an aerobics video. It seemed simple enough at the time. But, obviously, I wasn't prepared."

"Did your instructor think you were prepared?"

"Yes, but there was no way he could have known that I hadn't really got it. It wasn't until I nearly died that we both realized that learning had not taken place."

"Sounds like a seriously high-stakes test—a real killer," he winked.

"Not funny, Barnabas: that experience really shook me and, although I went on to dive in open water and even in some caverns and lakes, I never became really comfortable with the sport. Looking back now, I believe it is because I was never properly prepared."

"But no one else seemed to have had the problem," he added, pointing to the pool and the other divers. "Why was it different for you?"

"I don't know and neither did Larry—that was the instructor's name. He really didn't notice any of us in the class individually. I mean, if the classroom had been empty, I am not sure he would have changed his instructional delivery—what he taught or how he taught it. He never saw us as individuals. It was as if we, the learners, were superfluous to the teaching."

With that I stopped and under the blue, balmy skies of the north-western Caribbean, I suddenly understood why Barnabas had brought me back to this time and place in order to remember such an uncomfortable, unsuccessful learning experience.

Barnabas broke the silence with, "Let's take a boat ride."

"Wait!" I ran after him as he strode purposefully toward the dock. "I understand. I think I know the Second Promise and why I couldn't answer whether or not my students achieved their learning objectives today."

"That's good," he replied, "and you'll have a chance to tell me once we're underway. For now, throw me that line and jump in."

Before I had a chance to ask where we were going, Barnabas had the engine of a small dinghy humming and me pushing off from a wooden dock lined with an assortment of vessels. As we got out into the harbor, the familiar smell of the salt water was a welcome comfort after the harsh fumes of the chlorinated pool water. The little craft bounced gently over the light chop of the waves, bringing back pleasant memories of great open-water adventures like fishing, snorkeling, sailing, or just enjoying nature.

"So, tell me what you learned!" Barnabas shouted over the noise of the engine as he worked the tiller. "You said you thought you knew the Second Promise."

"Does it have something to do with how the teacher needs to learn about the student and to take responsibility for the student really getting it?" I asked.

"What do you mean?"

"Larry really knew his stuff and he was a great diver. I'm sure he must have taught that beginner scuba class over a hundred times. The problem was that he probably taught it exactly the same way each time—no matter who his students were."

"And what's wrong with that?" asked Barnabas as we exited the inlet at full throttle, skimming the clear blue sea and its colorful coral bounties.

"As you said, teaching and learning are not spectator sports. His teaching objectives were perfectly achieved at the expense of my learning objectives. He never allowed me to teach him how to teach me and, as a result, he never knew that I was unprepared to perform that skill.

"So what does that Principle, '*Teaching and learning are not spectator sports*,' have to do with you and the Second Promise to your students?"

"Not preparing students to read, write, and compute may not be life threatening, but these skills are still, in a different way, indispensable to survival." My throat closed with emotion at the thought of the untold numbers of children whose parents had not readied them for school, whose teachers had not prepared them for the next level of education, and whose children would be doomed to repeat the same vicious cycle of their parents' illiteracy.

As we increased our speed, Barnabas' white hair streamed back from his remarkably white face. He sat, one hand on the tiller and the other on his knee, keeping a constant eye on our heading.

"Go on," he encouraged.

"When we don't prepare our kids with the skills they need to be successful in the real world, we are dooming them to a life of dependence and poverty. Larry did not prepare me and I got into a really dangerous situation; but if I don't prepare my students, they too will be in compromised situations every day of their lives."

"So, tell me again," Barnabas coached. "What is it that this guy did not do to prepare you?"

"He didn't do what you are doing right now, what you have done from the moment I met you. He never took the time to learn from me how to teach me or to find out whether learning had taken place."

Barnabas smiled slightly with an approving nod. "Excellent! You have remembered the Second Promise: *I promise to learn from you how to teach you.*"

And when he said that, it was as if a huge hole had been filled in my understanding of teaching and learning—one that books and schools of education could not fill.

"Where are we going now?" I finally asked.

"Diving. We're going to get wet, of course."

Of course, I thought, of course. Teaching really is an adventure—an adventure steeped in exploration.

Barnabas and I didn't talk much for the rest of the trip. The dive was amazing with him as guide and teacher. For the first time since I donned a scuba tank, I felt comfortable in the water. On the way back home we flew low over the water following a family of dolphins. Unlike me, I mused, these amazing creatures were very well *schooled* at an early age in the art of diving.

When the little plane touched down, I felt as though I had been gone a lifetime.

"Thank you, Barnabas. Thank you for reminding me about the Second Promise: teaching objectives are important to have, but the real responsibility is in making sure students achieve their learning objectives. *The adventure of teaching is in exploring the ways my students learn and then discovering how to reach them, how to teach them, and how to test them.*"

"And the test for you?"

"Apply what I've learned: that's the real test." And as I said that, he turned into the small terminal of the airport.

"Wait, here is your flight cap." I ran after him, poking my head in through the door, but he was nowhere to be seen.

"The authority of those who teach is often an obstacle to those who want to learn."
Cicero

The next day was actually a teacher-planning day, so there were no students. It was probably a good thing for me because my adventures with Barnabas had left me a bit spent, both physically and emotionally. Except for my sore legs from diving and the cap from my flight, I might have questioned if yesterday's adventures had really occurred. The campus seemed empty without the young bodies dodging back and forth and without the boisterous voices reverberating throughout the hallways. Instead, an occasional teacher or two could be seen, casually clad, walking to or from the classrooms, sometimes stopping to chat with a colleague. I was still new and really didn't know anyone very well, so I was not a participant in any of the "teacher talk."

Before settling into a plan for carrying out the Second Promise, I decided to get a cup of coffee from the staff room. I was surprised to see how many teachers were in there, drinking coffee and chatting. One of the teachers greeted me and invited me to join them. I was really in a hurry and anxious to get back to my classroom, but I did not want to seem impolite so I stayed.

"How's it going?" she asked. But as I opened my mouth to respond she jumped in with, "Oh, I know it is hard the first year and you probably have the toughest students."

"Toughest students?" I was surprised by her assumption.

"Yes, administration always gives new teachers the problem kids, because you newbies are least likely to complain." She looked around at the other teachers knowingly and continued. "We more—seasoned—teachers just send the disruptive kids out of our classrooms on referrals and suspensions. The deans don't like all the extra paperwork, and then there are the parents who complain that their angels are being mistreated and misunderstood." The others marked their agreement with hushed laughter.

I think by now my mouth may have dropped open a centimeter or two, but the teacher didn't seem to notice.

"Not to worry, dear. In a few years they'll stop giving you the bad ones. Just remember to give out lots of referrals and suspensions, and don't take any guff."

If the previous day seemed like a dream, the present day was beginning to feel like a nightmare. I didn't know what to say. It was true, I had not felt completely in charge of my classes and there were some behaviors from the students that were not appropriate, but I had attributed that to my own inexperience rather than some insidious plot to funnel students with discipline problems into my classes.

"I'll remember that," I responded politely and began to excuse myself from the table.

"Well, just remember," she called after me. "Remember, this is as good as it gets."

"What do you mean?" I asked, turning back to the table of teachers who by then were grinning almost mockingly at my naivety.

"Today ... today is an example of what a great job this would be if it weren't for the students."

"Oh, yes," I responded, trying not to show my disgust or embarrassment. "I see what you mean." And with that I rushed out, deciding to keep a coffee pot in my room from then on.

Once safely inside the confines of my classroom, I was thankful to have escaped somewhat unscathed from such negative thinking. I couldn't help wondering, though, what had happened to those once well-meaning professionals. Had they forgotten why they were all there? Didn't they realize students are central to our business: students are the customers and learning must be the organizing principle of the school? It's the students and their families we are meant to serve, not the system or the institutions.

Promise # 1: I promise to teach YOU

Promise # 2: I promise to learn from YOU

how to teach YOU

As I tried hard to forget the ugliness of what had just happened and to remember the beauty of the day before, I wrote the Second Promise on my white board, just below the first: "I promise to learn from YOU how to teach YOU." Once again I wrote the YOU in all caps then entered Principle Two in my planner: *Teaching and learning are not spectator sports.* I tried to remember the conversation I had had with Barnabas, the one that brought me back to my scuba experience.

Barnabas had asked, "How do you know if you fulfilled the First Promise, I promise to teach you?" And then, "It sounds like you achieved your teaching objectives, but did your students achieve their learning objectives?" I had answered honestly that I really didn't know. So, in that regard, I was not unlike my scuba instructor who hadn't known that I was not going to be able to clear my regulator under ten feet of water. The thought was ghastly.

To fulfill the Second Promise, I needed to figure out how to learn from my students, how to reach and teach them, and then how to find out if their learning objectives were achieved. But, first, they needed to recognize and own their learning objectives; they needed to make the objectives theirs.

Getting to know you…

I looked out at the 20 or so empty seats and multiplied them by five for the five periods of students who sat in them each day. I had to get to know each one of them.

"How can I do that?" I said out loud and slumped back into my desk chair. "One at a time," the answer resounded in my head. "One at a time." *The student must be allowed to teach the teacher how to teach; reciprocally the teacher must learn from the student how to teach.* Finally, everyone must be a player. *Teaching and learning are not spectator sports.*

Just then, I heard my classroom door squeak open. Oh, no, it was one of the teachers coming to share more negativity. I braced myself while spinning in my chair to face the door.

I sighed with relief to see Barnabas. "You are such a welcome sight. I thought you might have been one of *them*."

"Them?"

"The teachers." I explained what I had learned in the staff room that day. "They could really use your help."

"They could, but they won't."

"What do you mean?"

"Do you remember what I told you about my job?"

"Yes. You said that your job is to know when someone really wants help, but most people don't believe they need help, so they don't get it. You also said that your job is to know when someone cares enough about another person that they want to make a difference."

"You have a good memory, New Teacher; so do you understand why I can't help your negative albeit omniscient colleagues?"

"They don't view themselves as being part of the problem; so they don't think they need help?"

"Right again. These are actually hard-working people in dysfunctional systems that have beaten them down into complacency and survival mode. They do what they must to get through the day."

The only thing that interferes with my learning is my education.

Albert Einstein

"Are you ready for another adventure? The Third Promise awaits."

"But I haven't applied the second yet."

"I know, that's okay: two and three go hand in glove. Besides, you've made a good start," he said pointing to the board and the mess of paper on my desk.

"How do you know that?"

As I asked the question, Barnabas leaned against the desk in a half-sitting position, picked up the flight cap, evidence of the previous day's adventures, and studied it with his fingers. *"The student must be allowed to teach the teacher how to teach; reciprocally the teacher must learn from the student how to teach. Finally, everyone must be a player."*

He was reading my thoughts again.

"I know," he confirmed. "Are you ready to go?"

I looked at all the books and ungraded papers on my desk. "What about all this?"

"You won't need any of that stuff where we are going."

"I mean, when will I get it all done? Teaching can be overwhelming you know. There is a part of me that can relate to the whining that goes on in the staff rooms of the world."

"It is only as complicated or 'overwhelming' as you make it. Contrary to what most people think, good teaching does not require martyrdom. I'll show you where some of the best teachers are having the time of their lives. Some of these teachers were yours."

"Mine?"

"Yes," he replied, as he drew a tiny circle in the air above his head. I had learned that hand motion the day before, in 60 feet of water: it meant we were leaving.

"Do I need this?" I called after him and held up the fraying flight cap.

"No, not today."

Although I had grown comfortable in the old biplane, I was relieved to be flying in a more conventional—no—contemporary manner. Nothing about my travels with Barnabas could be called "conventional."

"Here, take this." He pulled a newspaper clipping out of the front pocket of his plaid shirt as we walked toward the parking lot.

"Another cartoon?" I asked, remembering Barnabas' predilection for comics.

"I clipped this one thinking it would give you a chuckle— especially today."

He was right. It sure brought some levity to my earlier experience in the teachers' lounge. I thought about hanging it up there, if I could do so unnoticed, and wondered how my "seasoned" advisors would deal with Calvin. One thing was certain: Calvin would not have lasted long in one of their classes. I thought about how much fun he would be in mine and laughed out loud.

"Glad you enjoyed that. You can keep it or … place it where others can enjoy it, too." Barnabas winked and smiled broadly.

The old jeep was parked in the back parking lot.

"Wait," I said. "I forgot to sign out. I'm not really supposed to leave campus yet. It's a planning day."

"You will be planning. Don't worry, you won't be missed."

He was right about that. Teachers make up just a tiny blip on the system's radar screen—just a bit bigger than that of the students.

New Teacher

New teacher,
Young idealist
It is hard for you to fit in
With all your dreams and expectations

New teacher,
Light spirit
They don't want you here
You with your unjaded visions

New teacher,
Your energies unbridled
You are a danger here
In the safety of sameness

New teacher,
Beware
Hide your enthusiasm
Don't show them you care

New teacher,
Be wary
They frown on you
You, too new

goldenpair

Chapter 3

WHAT GETS IN THE WAY?

"Teaching can be compared to selling commodities. No one can sell unless someone buys... [yet] there are teachers who think they have done a good day's teaching irrespective of what the pupils have learned."

John Dewey

"Where's the biplane today?" I asked, as we pulled up to where the Cessna was waiting.

"She's getting some work done on 'er—needs a little attention before I can take her back up."

"Where did you say we were going?"

"I didn't. What I did say was that I'll show you where some of the best teachers are having the time of their lives—some of these teachers were yours. Do you remember when you first learned that you didn't always have to be in control to be successful, that letting go can be very powerful if you stay focused?"

"I'm not sure I ever really learned that, but might have experienced it once or twice. It's a very freeing feeling."

"Well, let's see if we can jog your memory." And the mighty Cessna took off into an amazingly blue sky—a sky decorated with puffy white clouds. As we raced by, I tried stretching my memory to the time that Barnabas had mentioned. I remembered the feeling, but not the event. Did it really happen? It seemed as elusive as the clouds we were passing.

"Would you like to do a little cloud skiing?" Barnabas intercepted my thoughts.

"Cloud what?"

"Cloud skiing," he repeated.

"Do we have to get out of the plane?" I asked with dread.

Barnabas looked over to me with a huge grin and then uncontrollable laughter shook his large frame. "No, of course not. Let me show you. Are you wearing your harness?"

"I've got my seat belt on."

"You need your harness, too." After helping me buckle up, he turned my world literally upside down and all around. Cloud skiing, as I came to find out, was Barnabas' description of circumnavigating the outermost edges of a cloud, which we did over and over until I believe we touched every outermost water molecule of its cotton-candy puffiness.

"You probably wouldn't want to do this with more than one plane to a cloud at the same time, would you?" he mused and flew us back on course.

Cloud skiing. What next, I thought?

"How do you feel?" he asked and looked over to where I sat next to him in the cockpit.

"Free," I managed to answer. "Very free, without a care in the world."

"Hold on to that feeling."

It may have been the rhythmic roar of the small craft's engine or the strenuous adventures of the previous day, but as I tried holding on to "that feeling," I fell sound asleep and had the most wonderful dream. I dreamed that I was back in the dance studio of my high school—a performing arts school. We were doing a turn combination in center floor exercises; I prepared for my turn and then stayed up to complete an uncountable number of revolutions. It was an amazing feeling to effortlessly spin and spin until I decided that that was enough—wow! I woke reluctantly as we touched down. Yet the dream stayed with me, and my mind drifted back to my days as a young high-school student studying to be in the theatre. We all worked hard because we knew when we got out, it would be very competitive. Jobs were few and far between, and only the really talented and/or lucky got work. The more I thought about those times, the more I realized that that was where I learned how to let go in order to make things happen.

"I think I remember now when it was that I was able to abdicate total control and still feel good about the end product."

"I thought you would. That cloud skiing does it every time—yes-err-e-Bob—every time."

Barnabas certainly had a way of turning my world upside down and all around—from cloud skiing to time travel. It was his way of getting me to see things from a new perspective, using the bifocal power of an electron microscope and a binocular telescope all in one.

"To fly as fast as thought, to anywhere that is, you must begin by knowing that you have already arrived…"

Richard Bach

"Oh, I loved this place! A part of me has never left. I learned so much here!" I exclaimed as Barnabas and I walked through the doors of my old high school. "But it moved from this location: it's not in this building anymore."

"Remember, I told you that you would see all things as they were when you first learned each of the Six Promises."

"Oh, that's right," I remembered. I would see all my old friends as they were then. "Look, there's Kathy; she's famous now—on Broadway. And Gene, there's Gene; he has a great ballet career! I wonder if Mrs. Shannon is in her English classroom. I'd love to see her again."

"Let's go to the place where you learned the art of letting go, of really digging down into your bag of creativity and ingenuity."

"Then we'll have to go this way to the drama department." I guided Barnabas down the halls that were embedded with so many memories. Our footsteps clicked on the polished floors as we followed familiarly worn paths.

"We're going to an improvisation class, aren't we?" I asked.

"Yes, you remember."

"It is amazing the resources you can find inside yourself when you visualize and just let go." While I stood watching myself as a young teenager perform an improvisation, I wondered where that spirit had gone. The performance was believable, yet there was no script. The words and actions were self-selected and directed. My drama teacher had set up the situation, but my partner and I worked together to engage the audience and make it real for them.

"What do you see going on there?" asked Barnabas.

"A lot of spirit and creativity. I really miss that: I miss the interaction with the audience. My teachers told me I had a special kind of connection that reached over the footlights. It was strange, but I could almost feel what the audience was feeling and thinking. As a result, I could change my performance to meet their needs. There was a kind of chemistry during a live performance that I have never been able to explain or duplicate. But what does any of this have to do with the Six Promises or at least Promises Two and Three?"

"Remember the Second Promise?"

"I promise to learn from you how to teach you."

"And how do you do that in a class of 20 or more?"

"One at a time and by allowing them to teach me how to teach them."

"Then what must you do once you have learned how to teach them?"

"I don't know."

"Look," he said. "Look at what you are doing there."

"But this is entertainment, not teaching. I don't understand."

"Are the two so different? You said that there was a chemistry that occurred in a live performance, which you could not explain—one that inspired you to do something a little different to reach your audience, an audience of perhaps hundreds. You also said yesterday that to fulfill the Second Promise, you needed to figure out how to learn from your students—*how to reach and teach them*—in order to find out if their learning objectives were achieved."

"That's different," I argued.

"The objectives are different, but the Promise is not," responded Barnabas calmly.

The voice of the drama teacher rose above the din of my thoughts, "Okay, now the situation has changed to include the arrival of your parents. Bring the scene to conclusion." That meant we had to "pretend" something new, invent on the fly, and still make our acting believable and meaningful to the audience—connect with them.

Improvisation is hard to explain to someone who has never labeled it as such, but most have experienced it at some point in their lives. Even folks locked into the strictest routines, by choice or not, must occasionally break away from the daily scripts of their lives. By virtue of our environment and fellow humans, we are called upon continuously to improvise. Some call it adaptation; others call it change or problem solving. In acting, it literally means performing without a script: the actors are given situational anchors from which they can play off one another as well as their audience. The difference between life and theatre, I supposed, is the ratio between actor and audience. In the theatre or any sort of performance/presentation situation, the ratio is one actor/communicator to however many persons in the audience. In the course of our daily lives, interpersonal communication generally occurs one-on-one. Any classroom of more than two or three students, therefore, is more like the theatre, I thought. So in that sense, I was beginning to see the similarities.

I heard my former voice rise above the laughter of the thirty or so students in the audience, as I spun a fantastic yarn for my skit parents in an attempt to avoid getting into major trouble. I noted the intuitive *changes* I made to capture my audience and keep them engaged, while the other actors and I brought the scene to conclusion. It was as though I were learning from the audience how to perform for them but also how to *change* my performance via improvisation to better connect with them. Barnabas was right: "The objectives are different, but the Promise is not." As the scene ended and my former classmates stood in applause, I whispered what I remembered to be the Third Promise. "*I promise to change my teaching based on what you have taught me.*"

Just as I had changed my acting to accommodate the directions of the drama teacher, the improvisation of my fellow actors, and the reactions of the audience, I would have to change my teaching to accommodate the responses of my students—and do so on an individual basis.

"Yes, yes, that's right and it addresses the Principle '*There can be no teaching without learning.*' Can you see now why Promises Two and Three are inseparable—as inseparable as performing and teaching?"

"Yes, in Promise Two the teacher learns how to teach the student. The continuation of that is in Promise Three—the promise to change teaching based on what the teacher has learned from the student." I felt the return of a long-lost love: performing. Of course, that had to be a part of what teaching and learning were all about: change, adaptation, and problem solving.

The theatre is a magic place where audience and performer communicate in subtle ways that are difficult to explain or analyze. The fact, however, that both audience and performer are changed by the experience of the performance (be it dance, music, drama, or comedy) is undeniable. Teaching and learning can also be magical—magical and meaningful when teacher and student are changed by the experience of the dialogue.

THERE CAN BE NO TEACHING WITHOUT LEARNING

"The biggest enemy to teaching is the talking teacher."

John Holt

When the jeep pulled up to the school, it seemed as though time had stood still. The gang of teachers that had been in the staff room was just moving en masse toward the classrooms. I looked down at my watch; barely a half-hour had gone by.

"See, I told you that you wouldn't be missed and you still have plenty of time for planning."

"Gee, thanks. Would you like to stay and help?"

"I'd love to, but I have another teacher who needs my help today." And with a wave and a wink, Barnabas sped off.

As I walked back to my classroom, I cordially greeted the teachers in passing, "How's the planning going?" Most responded in kind, passing by with little or no investment. Mrs. Smith, on the other hand, stopped to give me a little advice and to let me know she really did not need planning time as such; she was catching up on her reading.

"Oh?" I questioned. "Do you plan at home?"

"Heavens, no, dear. I did my plans years ago." Mrs. Smith was one of the most "seasoned" teachers at the school. The kids joked she had been there before the building; actually, they said the school was built around Mrs. Smith and her desk, which was always neatly arranged with two stacks of student worksheets— graded and ungraded. As she got closer to me, I could smell a sweet mixture of perfume and powder. The exaggerated movements of her red, glossy lips took on a life of their own as they pedantically shaped her words.

"Now, I just want to tell you—you being a new teacher and all that—if you plan well during the first couple of years and you get in good with the administration so they give you the same courses to teach every year ... well, you'll have those lesson plans until you get ready to retire. Then you can have your planning days to yourself to—you know—catch up on other things."

"You're so right, Mrs. Smith. Thanks for the tip." By this time, I was mercifully at my classroom door and could excuse myself. Pleased with her "good-deed for the day," Mrs. Smith sauntered back to her room and her desk from where she would continue to sit and deliver the same material, in the same way, to a myriad of indifferent students. As I watched her flowered frock disappear around a corner, I reflected on the events of the past two days and wondered how, contrary Mrs. Smith's advice, I would keep the Three Promises to my students—how my lessons would reflect the adventurer, explorer, and performer I had rediscovered.

I wrote the Third Promise on the whiteboard underneath the second: "I promise to change my teaching based on what YOU have taught me." Once again, "YOU" was written in all caps. I stood back and stared at the black letters against the starkness of the whiteboard until they began to take shape in my mind's eye. I wrote Principle Three in my plans: *There can be no teaching without learning!*

> ## Promise # 1: I promise to teach YOU
>
> ## Promise # 2: I promise to learn from YOU
>
> ## how to teach YOU
>
> ## Promise # 3: I promise to change my teaching
>
> ## based on what YOU have taught me.

I had already demonstrated commitment to the First Promise: I promise to teach YOU—*teach ALL students, no matter their learning style, level, or need.* The Second Promise, I promise to learn from you how to teach you, is simply a promise to *find out if learning has taken place and, if not, why.* The Third Promise, I promise to change my teaching based on what you have taught me, is another way of saying that *I am willing to do whatever it takes to make certain that learning has taken place.* Making the promises was easy; coming up with a systematic approach I could depend on to help me keep them—that was a challenge. I went back to the whiteboard and tried to imagine what Barnabas would say if he were here. Finally, I began writing:

1. *Identify*—discover objectives that students need and want to achieve
2. *Teach*—reach out to all students by being a performer, a communicator who gets and holds their attention
3. *Test*—watch, listen, formulate unique questions for each student by being an explorer, an adventurer
4. *Learn*—change how you teach by being an improviser, a creator

And then, if needed, do it all again and again by doing whatever it takes to achieve the learning objective.

Four short steps—it seemed too simple. But Barnabas said it didn't have to be complicated, and martyrdom was certainly not required for teaching to be effective. The real test was if the four steps really and consistently worked. So I thought about ways in which I could apply the process.

The students had already responded to my questions regarding their writing samples—questions that invited them to make realistic assessments of their reading and writing, and from which a dialogue with each of them had begun. Through our written conversations, I was really getting to know them.

It would naturally follow to mutually decide on areas in which they wished to improve. **Step 1**—*Identify* objectives that students need and want to achieve. Once the individual learning objectives were established, I would be able to plan out strategies to: **Step 2**—*Teach* by creating a contagious excitement and by finding multiple ways to reach all students. While teaching, I would find ways to continually: **Step 3**—*Test* whether or not learning had taken place by watching, listening, and asking questions. In that way I could: **Step 4**—*Learn* how and when to change my teaching. Thus I could, if needed, **Identify—Teach—Test—Learn again and again**—as many *different* times as necessary. Trusting in my improvisational and problem-solving abilities would be the key to doing whatever it took for my students to achieve their learning objectives.

When the first class of students arrived, they saw the three Promises prominently displayed on the whiteboard. Under that were the words: Identify Teach Test Learn Identify Teach Test Learn Identify Teach Test Learn... The written promises were for my students; the repeated sequence of "identify, teach, test, learn" (ITTL) was a reminder to me of the four steps I had to follow.

As I waited for the proverbial curtain to go up on the first class, I had a healthy bout of stage fright and self-doubt. But then I remembered Larry, the less-than-responsible scuba instructor who had nearly drowned me, and my misgivings were quickly dispelled. I had to keep the Promises and this was the best way I knew how.

At first, the four steps seemed awkward, but as I kept my focus on the students and their learning needs, I was able to learn more about how to help them achieve their learning objectives. Each time I thought I was unable to motivate or coach a student toward his or her goal, I would ask the student what he/she thought a good solution might be. And each time it was the student who forced me to think innovatively and consider alternative teaching methods. What worked for one student rarely worked for another. My ideas were never as good as those of the students themselves, and if I could help a student really identify the problem, then the two of us could solve it together.

One such situation occurred with one of my graduating senior girls. When I first read Lynette's writing sample, all I could see was the poor structure and muddy meaning. A closer look revealed her flair for descriptive words and phrases; there was feeling in her writing. When I asked Lynette to assess her work and tell me what she wanted to learn, she was not able to hone in on the areas that needed improvement; however, she was able to express a desire to write youth news articles for her church bulletin. Perfect! Writing news articles of any kind requires a precise structure and presentation of the facts. **Step 1**, identification of learning objectives completed, we continued to **Step 2**: I needed to find the best way to teach Lynette the simple "who, what, when, where, how" formula for writing news. I provided her a model news article she could follow when writing a piece with a topic of her own choosing—perhaps one about her last youth group activity. But her first attempt to apply the model—**Step 3**—proved unsuccessful. I learned—**Step 4**—that a simple model was not enough for Lynette: it did not produce the results we wanted, which was a news article that presented the facts in a clear, well-organized fashion. So she and I discovered a different way to achieve her learning objective to write clear, well-organized facts. Another student in her class was very strong in the area of organizing clear, factual thoughts but not particularly expressive with his use of language. Leigh had applied several times to the school newspaper but was not accepted. His learning objective was to bring life to his writing. Both students agreed to work together and learn from each other's strengths and weaknesses. Lynette's writing began to improve in leaps and bounds: she published her first article in the church bulletin that very month. Leigh's writing became so much more colorful and interesting that after Lynette and I encouraged him to reapply to the school paper, he was accepted to cover all club activity news.

The ITTL process worked to uncover students' skill gaps, of which there were many. Skills and knowledge, which students had managed to feign over the years, were now being revealed in their true light, and an unexpected bi-product of ITTL surfaced among the students soon after I introduced it. One day, I noticed some of my students lingering after the last bell, and I could overhear that they wanted to ask me something. Finally, the group approached, led by one brave student who asked:

"Are you going to do this all year?"

"Am I going to do what all year?" I was confused by the question.

They looked at one another until one of them finally blurted out, "Get so … well … get to know us so well. You know, up close and personal."

I still wasn't sure I understood what they meant. "Do you mean am I going to continue to learn more about you?"

The spokesperson for the group nodded affirmatively.

"Well, sure." I looked at the concern on their faces. It was as though they were being forced to reveal some deep dark secret. "I need to know what you want to learn, what you need to learn, and the best way to teach you. Isn't that okay?"

"It's just that none of our other teachers did that and … well some things you think are important … we didn't learn them."

"What are you afraid of?" I finally asked, noticing the dread in their eyes.

Another student, a tiny girl, who had remained in the back of the group volunteered, "We think you're going to give us bad grades when you find out all the stuff we can't do, and we won't be able to graduate."

Where was Barnabas when I really needed him? What was this Pandora's Box I had inadvertently opened? Understandably, my students were concerned that someone, perhaps for the first time, was uncovering their dirty secrets: all the skills and knowledge that had not been properly acquired. I didn't know what to say except to try to allay their fears of bad grades and promise to continue to teach them.

"Don't you want to read and write really well so that you can—"

"Pass this class and graduate?" the girl finished my question.

"No, so you can get good jobs—ones that you like and have chosen—and go on to college if you want. I will make you a promise now that is not written on the board. I promise that if you continue to teach me how to teach you, neither one of us will get bad grades. You will graduate and I will keep my job." They seemed somewhat satisfied that I was telling the truth and that their secrets were safe with me. I would not betray them or judge them harshly for their inadequacies. But what about all the others who did not have the courage to ask me whether I was going to continue to be "up close and personal"? The last thing I needed was adolescent anxiety interfering with learning.

After the students left, I started cleaning up. I thought I had kept the Promises, but the old adage "no good deed goes unpunished" kept rummaging around in my brain. I had not expected what I had found: most of my students were not at grade level and some were functionally illiterate. It saddened me to think of the lost teaching and learning opportunities that had been permitted to occur over their young lives. Once again, the job seemed impossible, this time for a different reason.

After an obsessively long cleaning frenzy and some notes for the next day, I lingered a bit over the daily newspaper, hoping to share the day's events with Barnabas. I imagined him with another new teacher off on some adventure while I leafed through the day's news. Following Barnabas' lead, I skipped quickly to the comics and oddly found Calvin and Hobbs with a message clearly reflective of my day's experiences. I could not help thinking that Barnabas had somehow had a hand in even that.

Still no Barnabas, I picked up my evening's work, locked the door behind me and headed to my car. As I began to back out of my parking space, I could see the familiar jeep in my rear-view mirror. Barnabas pulled up in the space next to me and breathlessly summoned me to get in. It was getting late and I wasn't sure I was up to whatever he had in mind. He seemed in a big hurry.

"Come on," he called impatiently. "No time for chit chat. We've got to hurry."

"Men learn while they teach."

Lucius Annaeus Seneca

goldenpair

Chapter 4

A WAY TO TEACH

"Some people have greatness thrust upon them, very few have excellence thrust upon them."

John W. Gardner

As usual, he got his way and I found myself obediently locking my car door and jumping into the seat next to him. This was out of character for Barnabas; he was usually methodical and laid back.

"Are we late for a train?" I asked jokingly.

"No," he answered. "A ship."

"A ship?"

"Yes, we've got to board the cargo ship called Avgi (Dawn) that is leaving from the harbor at sunset."

"Cargo ship Avgi … I worked on that ship one summer in between under-graduate semesters."

"Yes, I know. That's why we're going. Promise number four awaits—remember?"

I could not believe it was nearly night, and we were racing off to catch an old Liberty ship, which, if it hadn't by then, should have been scrapped. It was falling apart when I sailed her as an assistant radio officer.

"Barnabas, are you sure we need to do this now—tonight?" The look I got in response to my question spoke volumes. It said: "Would I be doing this if I didn't have to?" and "There is much to be learned, so quit whining."

We were losing the light with every mile that raced past, and the wind got increasingly chilly. I buttoned my sweater and pulled the collar closer up around my neck.

"How much farther?" I asked.

"We're here," he shot back and turned sharply into a gravel-filled parking area set back from a small harbor. There was the Avgi as I remembered her several years ago in that very port. Barnabas jumped out of the jeep, and I followed close behind. There was no sense in asking questions. I had learned by then that I would know what I needed to know when I needed to know it. I just could not imagine what the Fourth Promise had to do with this old cargo ship.

"They are waiting for us to push off," he said.

A rope ladder—the only way onboard—hung down from the ship's gunnel, which rose about 30 or 40 feet above the waterline. The ship must have just begun loading as she was still high in the water, just like the first time I saw her at that very dock. We approached the bottom rung of the ladder, which swung slightly in the wind. Barnabas took hold of it and gestured for me to start the climb. I remembered the first time I had climbed that ladder, thinking this "adventure" might not have been such a good idea after all. But the shipping company had already paid my travel to that God-forsaken spot and I did not have the funds to pay them back. So it was up the 40-foot swinging ladder, while carrying a summer's worth of belongings. That was only the beginning of more escapades than I had bargained for—an experience of a lifetime.

"What are you waiting for?" Barnabas coaxed.

"I don't see the top—I don't see the deck." From where I stood, perched on the bottom rung, the ladder seemed to go on forever into what looked like half-lit clouds. The deck landing was nowhere in sight.

"You will, you'll see—just climb."

We started our climb, I in front and he following close behind. I kept a death-grip on the ladder ropes. The smell of limestone dust and salty sea air brought me back to that eventful summer during which I found a way to fulfill my need for an adventure and to see more of the world than I could ever have on a student's budget. For that, all I had to do was help the radio officer. It was a match made in heaven, or so it seemed.

"Are we really going to sail with her?" I shouted back to Barnabas above the din of the loading machinery as we balanced ourselves precariously on the rickety planks of the old ladder.

"That depends," he shot back. With that, our ascent somehow dizzyingly translated itself into a sudden arrival—I was getting quite accustomed to these flashy exhibits of Barnabas' skills—in the communication office, where we found the radio officer and, of course, my younger self.

"What do you remember most about your experiences aboard the Avgi?" Barnabas asked above the roar of the loading machinery.

"I remember being challenged beyond my wildest imagination."

"In what way?"

"In every way."

"Go on."

"I'd never been on a ship before, so just getting around the vessel with its steep stairwells and gangplanks, was challenging. The Avgi was no cruise ship—no modern conveniences or amenities. It was a Greek-owned and - operated cargo ship, which should have been scrapped years before. My ticket on board was my claim to being of Greek descent and knowing both Greek and English. However, knowing Greek and being fluent, which was expected of me, were two different things. I tell you, my Greek improved exponentially: it had to! I was also expected to participate in all the safety drills and "all hands on deck" during emergencies, which occurred frequently. In the three months I was onboard, we lost the use of all navigational devices, our foghorn, our short-wave radio, and other minor pieces of equipment. The deck officers used sextants to navigate; the radio officer was relegated to the use of long-wave radio only; and the one time we were in dense fog, all hands were on deck banging pots and pans to announce our anchored position in an inland waterway. Yes, I would say there were a few challenges."

"And the result?"

"As I said, my Greek improved; I learned to keep my head in emergencies; and I gained confidence in my ability to take care of myself in the face of danger."

"Why do you think you didn't buckle under pressure? It sounds like you were under a good deal of pressure most of the time."

"My expectations of myself were high, and there were others depending on me to do my job and to do it well. What started out as a lark and a holiday turned out to be a serious education in life skills. I couldn't just give up or give in to mediocrity."

Barnabas and I observed as the radio officer familiarized my younger self with the equipment in the tiny office cabin. We listened as the officer gave instructions at a mile-a-minute in Greek. I watched myself strain to understand everything he said and then hunker down to ready myself for the challenges that were about to befall me. Over the crude and crackly public announcement system, I could hear the familiar sounds of the crew readying the ship for departure.

"Did you have any fun that summer?" Barnabas pressed me.

"Are you kidding! I wouldn't have exchanged that adventure for a year-long cruise on the Queen Elizabeth II. Are we going to stay on board? The next stop will be Trinidad, you know. That could pose a problem for the application of the next promise."

Ignoring my question Barnabas asked, "Have you remembered the promise yet?"

I thought back to the small band of courageous students who had expressed their concern over possible poor grades and being held back Then I thought about the expectations that their previous teachers had had for them versus the ones I held. I wondered for the first time what their expectations were of themselves. Were they up for the challenges my class would bring? I already promised them that I would do my best to help them do their best so...

"It has to do with high expectations and the promise to do my best in order to help my students do their best," I said. "I was really fortunate to be placed in a situation here that had built-in high expectations. There was no hiding from failure: if I screwed up, people noticed. In contrast, my students have been allowed to hide behind a veil of teaching and learning excuses. They have been victims of unpronounced promises. I think the Fourth Promise is: *I promise to do my best to get you to do your best.*"

"Good, yes, and the Principle that you already stated is that…"

"*Expectations Count,*" I added.

"Well done, New Teacher. I guess we don't need to stay on board after all." And, before I knew it, we were in Barnabas' jeep racing back to my school.

EXPECTATIONS COUNT

When the jeep pulled in next to my car, I didn't get in. Instead I headed back to my classroom.

"Where are you going?" Barnabas called after me.

"I've got a promise to keep," I called back.

Once back in my room I wrote the Fourth Promise beneath the other three: "I promise to do my best to get YOU to do your best." Once again the word "YOU" was written in caps. I stood back knowing full well how I would keep that promise, and then circled Principle Four in my planner: *Expectations Count!*

Promise # 1: I promise to teach YOU

Promise # 2: I promise to learn from YOU

how to teach YOU

Promise # 3: I promise to change my teaching based

on what YOU have taught me

Promise # 4: I promise to do my best to get YOU

to do your best

When you set the achievement bar high, you run a higher risk of failure. No one likes to fail. So, when teachers' expectations are low, is it because they are being realistic or is it because they do not want to risk failure? And whose failure concerns them more—the students' or their own? I wasn't certain of the answers to any of these questions, but I was resolved to set the learning bar high for my students. To get them to do their best, I would have to do my very best, and it would not be easy.

In addition, I had not resolved the problem of how to reassure my students that their academic weaknesses offered opportunities for improvement and not necessarily for failure. These young people had been beaten down by a dysfunctional system—a vicious cycle devoid of accountability, a cycle in which the students were almost always the losers.

Could I really break this cycle? It is said that a journey of a thousand miles must begin with a single step. The challenge was in taking that first step. How could I continue to teach, test, and learn more about my students without intimidating them? How could I encourage them to do their best and continue to raise the achievement bar?

Thoughts of the Avgi came back to me and of how I too had felt intimidated and inadequate when I first joined the crew. However, I was fortunate in that I had someone who encouraged me to "hang in" and do my best. The radio officer, who was my boss, explained that if I did less than my best—whatever the outcome of my efforts—I would not feel good about myself. Similarly, if I tried to do more than my best, I would spend more energy than was needed, leading to feelings of not having done enough. So the key was "doing my best" and to do so for the pleasure of it. The motivation for doing my best needed to come from intrinsic rather than extrinsic rewards.

I thought about that inner process as it related to my students; I considered the conversations I had with the few who were brave enough to talk about their fears of failing and their concerns about getting poor grades and of not graduating. Their motivations for doing their best were extrinsic. Then I thought about the often subjective and arbitrary ways in which we grade and are graded. What criteria do we use, what methods? Does the grading system provide students with the information they need to improve their learning? Does it encourage them to do better—"their best"—intrinsically, or does it discourage with deprecating labels?

The way in which I graded students was the way in which I was graded as a student. When I really analyzed it, the objective of my grading system was more about categorizing and judging than about teaching and learning. I therefore decided to commit myself to changing the way in which I provided feedback to a method that would encourage students to intrinsically want to do their best. The method was a simple one: *grades would be based on both achievement and on improvement—on students doing their best.* Knowing my students and evaluating them individually would be the key to using this new grading system.

I looked at the ungraded papers that were left on my desk before Barnabas swept me off to the harbor and was glad I had not yet got to them. I examined each with a new eye and new criteria: *improvement.* After evaluating as I had always done according to the standards and criteria, I graded the students based on their individual growth—their performance of a given skill compared to their past performance of the same skill. The final grade was a composite of the two scores.

When I had finished, I was amazed at the grade distribution and rankings. Students who had been receiving low scores based on skill level alone, received much higher grades when improvement was factored into their assessment. I was excited about the effect this would have on their motivation to continue to improve. However, there were also cases of students whose grades did not improve: some of these already had good skills. This told me two things: one was that the old grading system did not provide them with the feedback they needed to reach the next level, and the second was that I had not adequately applied ITTL to help those students achieve more advanced learning outcomes.

So, in addition to helping my students do their best, I found that this new grading system held me more accountable to doing my best. That is, I really had to understand each student's prior performance in order to provide an improvement grade. It was twice the work for me initially but, in the long run, it had really positive consequences. Some students, those involved in athletics, would later say the improvement grades were like receiving their personal times after a race. They were able to keep track of their outcomes and compete with themselves in order to strive for their next "personal best." So, in a nutshell, the improvement grades were a great measurement tool for both teacher and learner, providing "personal best" results on an ongoing basis. This was real accountability. I left the school that evening tired but content and looking forward to sharing the new grading system with my students and passing back the papers, which for the first time reflected a mark of their achievement as well as their improvement.

"I am beginning to suspect all elaborate and special systems of education. They seem to me to be built on the supposition that every child is a kind of idiot who must be taught to think."

Anne Sullivan

The next day, as students took their seats, opened their notebooks and texts, and made themselves comfortable, I couldn't help but think what a different atmosphere this was than the manic, out-of-control environment at the beginning of the school year. My classroom was beginning to be a place of shared vision, trust, and love.

I passed back the students' papers and explained the new grading system. At first, it appeared really foreign; but as they learned more about how it would help them keep track of their progress toward their goals, the students became more comfortable. Students who had been initially concerned about the harmful outcome of exposing inadequate skills, were now reassured that being realistic was in their best interest, both long and short term. With the new grading system, they would be rewarded for improvement at any level. I also reaffirmed that my expectations of ALL of them were high, that their successes were my successes, and that we were in this teaching and learning thing together.

The feedback system for evaluation I set in place challenged students whose skills were already good, while giving hope to students whose skills were lacking. But, more importantly, it was a useful measurement tool for monitoring progress. In other words, it was an accountability system that could drive my instruction decisions.

goldenpair

Chapter 5:

A WAY TO LEARN

"It should be possible to explain the laws of physics to a barmaid."

Albert Einstein

By the end of the day, I was feeling pretty good about myself. A few students came up to me and thanked me for being fair, caring, interesting, etc.—all the things a new teacher wants to hear and needs for encouragement. I was so self-satisfied that I nearly forgot there were still two more Promises to remember (as Barnabas put it) and keep. Did I really need them anymore? And just as I was considering that question, Barnabas strolled through the door, newspaper in hand, and a smile on his face.

"Did you see this one?" he asked as he pointed to a cartoon from the local daily paper. It really speaks volumes about … well … here, you look." Barnabas placed the open newspaper in front of me on my desk.

As I looked over the cartoon, Barnabas laughed uncontrollably. "Genius, that's what it is, pure genius!"

I understood Barnabas well enough by then to know he hadn't brought that cartoon just to entertain me. No, he was always teaching, always had something for me to learn, and was always looking for the teachable moment. The cartoon was funny, but it made me feel defensive. What was he trying to say? Was this a criticism? He hadn't really seen my application of Promises Two, Three, and Four. He didn't know about all my successes and the fact that I was really making headway with my students. We were comfortable with one another: there was trust, engagement on their part, and encouragement on mine.

"I guess we all pay one way or another when students don't learn." Barnabas picked back up on the cartoon.

I had trouble responding but managed a polite, "Yes, I suppose we do," and changed the subject. "I've been having lots of success applying the Promises."

"I know."

"How ... how do you know?" I stuttered.

"I check in now and then."

"Check in?"

"With your students," he qualified.

"My students! You talk to my students?"

"Of course. How else would I know how you're doing?"

"Well, you could ask me, for a start," I replied indignantly.

"Yes, and that would give me part of the answer, but it is the students who count in this equation. Don't you think?"

He looked at me with that iridescent gleam in his eyes that could see right through the fluff. Barnabas had this uncanny ability to cut to the chase and weed out any illogical thinking. He was right, and I felt a little ashamed that I had changed my focus even for an instant from the students to myself.

Reading my thoughts again, Barnabas went on, "You may feel like you are succeeding and really making headway with your students. You may even be getting comfortable with them. You may feel they trust you, and you are engaging and encouraging them. All that is good, but the real question is: are they learning? To answer that, I go to the students. Oh, and by the way, did you realize Luis can't read?" and he went back to perusing the comics.

My face felt so flushed that he must have seen how embarrassed I was to have been so wittily exposed.

"I know he's been turning in assignments and taking the quizzes you've been giving, but have you noticed that it isn't his own work? Have you heard him read, or spent any one-on-one time with him?"

I immediately realized I hadn't. The times I had set aside for one-on-one with Luis had not occurred, but I could not remember exactly why. I picked up my planner that had been left open on my desk and paged through it. Barnabas was right: he had fallen through the cracks. Initially, I wanted to argue that it wasn't possible for him to come this far in school without being able to read, but I knew better than to doubt Barnabas.

"How ... how has this happened?" I stammered.

"It's simple: Luis' teachers made assumptions, the way you did. They believed that because he was a particular age and in a particular class, he had particular skill levels."

"That must mean they did not identify his learning needs then teach, test, learn, and teach again—ITTL!" I accused.

"Probably, but even if they had, they would have been unwilling or unable to define the missing teaching unit."

"What do you mean by 'teaching unit'?"

"*A teaching unit is the smallest possible piece of an idea, concept, or skill that can be tested with one simple question and answered with one simple answer, leaving no doubt that the student understands.* It can even be an "I've got it" look, but you'd need to know the student really well and be paying excellent attention..."

"So, because of those missing 'teaching units,' Luis now lacks the fundamental knowledge that he would need to build new skills?" I questioned.

"That's a good way to put it. Remember what you discovered at the start of our journey about your young students with visual disabilities being able to apply fundamental concepts to more complex ones?"

"Sure—that Vulcan 'mind melds' don't work because *part of learning is learning*."

"Right, and Luis missed the most fundamental 'teaching units'—the basic tools he needs to continue to learn."

"But, at this point, how can I find out what they are?"

"The challenge is in making 'questions' beautiful. You may not start out by testing the smallest teaching unit, but if you fail to get the desired answer, the piece isn't small enough, or your assessment question is not beautiful enough. There must be beauty in all of this."

"I'm still not sure I understand. What does beauty have to do with anything?"

"Ask me my name."

"What?"

"Ask me my name," he pressed.

"Okay. What's your name?"

"Barnabas," he answered. "Is it clear to you that I know the answer to your question?"

"Yes."

"So then what does that tell you about the question?"

I thought for a moment and then replied, "It tells me that the piece of the concept was small enough and the question was," I stopped and questioned, "beautiful enough to evoke the correct response?"

"Perfect!" he shouted, raising his arms over his head. "That's it! Now let's go. Sometimes the job is NOT possible, unless, of course, you have the right tools. Promise Five is waiting."

"Train?" I asked, shaking my head as we walked out the door.

"Train?" he asked and stopped to look at me.

"We've taken every other mode of transportation—that is, short of a space vehicle." His silence and whimsical glance worried me. "No, we're not!" I exclaimed and stood dead in my tracks.

Barnabas laughed out loud and looked at his watch. "No, where we are going does not require space travel, but it does require vision and is literally out of this world."

As we got into his jeep, he asked, "If you had one wish right now to make your teaching better, what would it be? What is the thing with which you are having the most difficulty?"

I had to stop and think about that one. I had been on such a high and feeling so good about everything, that I wasn't sure.

"I don't know," I replied.

"What about Luis? Think about Luis. How did he 'fall through the cracks,' as you put it?"

"I guess I just didn't catch—discover—go back far enough to the fundamentals with him."

"That's exactly right. Why not?"

"I'm not sure, but I feel as though I can't identify learning needs, teach, test, and learn fast enough."

"What do you mean?"

"Well I figured out that to apply the first three promises, I needed to **1)** *Identify* a learning objective that the students can own. Then I begin instruction or **2)** *Teach*; the next step **3)** is to *Test* by watching, listening, and asking questions of the students to ensure that learning has taken place; then, if needs be, **4)** I *Learn* how to change my teaching in order to be more successful; and, finally, I reiteratively *Teach again and again*, by doing whatever it takes to achieve the learning objective."

"Great. So you're saying that it's difficult to do that fast enough?"

"Yes, especially with so many students who are all at different levels and have different learning needs. In fact, it's virtually impossible. No wonder Luis got left behind, and he is probably not the only one."

"You're right, he isn't."

"I've been in la-la-land, haven't I? I'm no further along in this teaching and learning thing than I was when you first walked into my classroom."

"Not true!" Barnabas said emphatically. "You have gained great insight into being a good teacher. Your four-step approach is excellent. Right now, you need better tools and the skills to use them. I'm going to take you to a place where you will see what is possible when you've got the right technology, where you will experience the Principle of 'Learning Fast'"

"Where are we going?" I asked and laid my head back against the seat, letting the wind blow past my face and through my hair.

"The future," he answered. "We're going to the future."

I turned and looked at his purposeful expression and knew he was serious. Barnabas looked back at me with a smile.

"It is a future where students control the speed at which they learn because the technology learns from them how to teach them and at what speed. Just like your four steps, if the speed at which you present the next teaching unit depends on how fast you can learn from the student then *speed is limited by learning; learning is known by testing and testing is the fuel for speed.*"

"Yes, that's it. That's what I haven't been able to do," I said and sat bolt upright, causing my seat belt to lock hard against me.

"So, now I'll go back to my original questions: if you had one wish right now to make your teaching better, what would it be?"

"A way to find just the right questions and in just the right time— beautiful questions for every subject, every concept, every skill, every fact, and tailored for every student!" I exclaimed.

LEARN FAST

"The pursuit of truth and beauty is a sphere of activity in which we are permitted to remain children all our lives."

Albert Einstein

I closed my eyes and tried to imagine what such a learning environment would look like. Would it be a virtual reality with artificial intelligence to guide the students; would there be the need for a teacher? I was lost in contemplation when Barnabas turned into the driveway of what looked like an old, one-room schoolhouse.

"Where is this place?" I asked and looked around. I had not really kept track of the route, but from the short, what seemed like 20-minute drive, I thought it had to be in town. Yet I did not recognize where we were.

"Remember, I said we would go to the future? This is what a classroom could be, anywhere, anytime and for ALL students."

He parked, and I followed him to the door. As we approached, the door opened and a young woman emerged.

"Hi Barnabas," she greeted him. "It's so good to see you again. I see you've brought a visitor."

Barnabas introduced me as a promising new teacher who was anxious to see their teaching and learning environment.

"This is Loren, who will show us around today," he explained, as he held his hand over what looked like a scanning device.

"Will you sign in, please?" she asked, as she directed me to the device Barnabas had used. My quizzical look caught her attention, and she explained the scanner was a way of capturing the fingerprints of visitors and students alike:

"A quick and easy way to keep track of who's who."

"Wow! This would certainly be an easy way to keep attendance," I remarked.

"You're right: it definitely is!" Loren replied. "We use it for that, too, even though actual attendance here is not mandatory."

I looked at Barnabas and he noticed the surprise on my face.

"That's right," he said. "There will be many things here that will surprise you. This is not your mother's classroom."

"Come on," beckoned Loren. "Let me show you around."

I could not be certain if the outside of what seemed like a very small building was just deceptive, or whether the space inside the building expanded exponentially by some supernatural power, but the place was huge and looked nothing like a classroom or school or anything I had ever seen before. In fact, it looked a bit like the inside of a shopping mall, except that where the stores would be, there was an astonishing variety of learning environments. For example, there was an area that looked like a small meadow, another like a commercial kitchen; there was a medical center; a factory-looking setting; workshops, studios, labs, and a theatre. The number of areas went on as far as the eye could see.

"How many of these, these—" I wasn't sure what to call them—they were so amazing.

"You mean our *Applied Learning Environments*," said Loren, helping me describe the learning and teaching resources that seemed to go on forever. "We have as many as we need."

"I don't understand."

"When a student needs an environment in which to apply learning, we provide it. *Learning Environments* that go unused for one reason or another get converted into ones that are in demand," Loren clarified.

"What causes an *Applied Learning Environment* to lose or gain demand?" I questioned

"It has to do with business and industry. Students need to learn things today they did not need to know about ten years ago and vice versa."

"But how are you able to afford to make so many changes?" I asked.

"How can we afford not to?" she quickly responded. "Our students depend on us to prepare them for the real world with real-world skills. Business and industry depend on us to give them employees ready to work. Higher education depends on us to give them students ready for post-secondary education."

While her answer was so foreign to my experiences as a high-school teacher, it made such good sense and reminded me of a joke I once heard about Rip Van Winkle. After waking in a twenty-first-century business from a 300-hundred-year sleep, Rip was very confused because nothing looked familiar. To mitigate his nightmarish, anxious feelings he forced himself back to sleep only to wake a few hours later in a classroom of the same time period. He noticed that nothing had changed in the past 300 years and therefore felt quite comfortable. I could not help thinking that my students also notice the difference between the "real-world" and what goes on in their schools. Rather than making them comfortable like Rip Van Winkle, their education makes them want to go to sleep because it is not relevant to their lives.

As I strolled through this fantastic array of learning environments, I found it difficult to distinguish between the teachers and the students. There were computer stations everywhere, and most students and teachers carried pocket-sized devices that Loren explained were lightweight, low-cost, secure, durable, Internet-connected, e-mail-ready, wireless-network-enabled, peripheral-friendly, memory-rich, expandable computers, with phone, camera and electronic sensors/probes for scientific data collection. Whew!

Large flat-screen displays were strategically mounted to walls within each of the various environments, and the students/teachers seemed sometimes to be working in small groups and at other times one-on-one. Everyone was very engaged in whatever it was they were doing, and while, at first glance, it seemed informal and a bit chaotic, a closer look revealed a high level of structure. Some people stood; others were seated around tables; and still others were comfortably reading or using laptops in armchairs and couches scattered throughout the facility.

"Come on, there is an interesting class going on in here." Loren motioned me to enter a space that looked a bit like the inside of a movie theatre. "They're studying anatomy and physiology." With head-mounted displays, data gloves, and navigation tools, students were immersed in individual exploration.

"Is that virtual reality—VR?" I asked.

"Yes" Loren replied. "It is immersive VR. The students are getting their own personal tour today through the circulatory system. They can stop and visit anywhere they like and back track if they choose. They are getting a physical and intellectual experience impossible in the real world. If they have questions about anything they see, or if they get lost, there is an on-board guide that ·swers their questions."

"What does the teacher do? In fact, where is the teacher?" I questioned, looking around.

"Oh, she is right over there." Loren pointed to a slight, grey-haired woman standing at a computer station, immersed in a program and wearing headsets that looked like they came out of a recording studio.

"What is she doing?" I suppressed a laugh at the thought that the teacher could be listening to music and playing a computer game while her students were tripping through Hemoglobin City.

Barnabas shook his head and shot me a sideways glance and a wink. "She's a bit like the Wizard in the Wizard of Oz," he answered for Loren.

"That's a great way of putting it, Barnabas. Lucy is able to see everywhere the students are going and everything they do during their virtual trip, including the questions they ask. She also has the capability of challenging their voyage."

"What do you mean?"

"She can create road blocks."

"Like a blood clot?" I asked.

"Right, and force the students to take a detour. They have to figure out a different route to where they are going. Or she may set up tasks for them to do en route."

"Tasks?"

"Yes, for example, in the circulatory system she may ask the students to collect data about cholesterol, blood pressure, plaque, volume, etc."

"They are able to calculate all of that?"

"All of that and more," added Barnabas.

Remembering the genesis of our journey into the future and my frustration at not being able to identify student-learning needs, teach, test, and learn fast enough, I wondered how the technology helped Lucy to do that. How did it assist her in making decisions about instruction and about what tasks to set up for her students? How did it help her to quickly know when to move to the next task and then how to determine students' performance? I turned to Barnabas, who, of course, already had the answer.

"Systems like these are trained to evaluate and guide students as they work through problems," Barnabas responded. "They are programmed by using models."

"I'm not sure I understand what you mean."

This time Loren interjected: "For example, the system may learn from the intellectual behavior of a student working on a math problem, or it could be programmed with a range of pre-scored essays from which the system can evaluate and instruct."

The possibilities made my head spin as she continued, "There is around-the-clock access to evaluation and feedback. Of course, that gives the learners (teacher and student) increased scoring reliability and efficiency. Would you like to move on?" Loren invited.

"Yes, please," I agreed but wished I could join the class on their pulmonary journey—or even better—be the teacher facilitating the journey. As we walked to the next learning environment, I imagined ways I could use such tools in my archaic classroom.

"This system," I remarked, "it's like a personal coach."

"Exactly, one that offers hints when students stumble in the problem-solving process, not just when they enter an answer. As you can imagine, this kind of direct, intuitive instruction has a huge impact on student performance," Loren qualified.

"So why do you even need a teacher?" I asked.

"You can't replace a teacher." Barnabas jumped in.

"The system is merely a tool directing human contact where it's most needed." Loren explained. "I'll give you an example. Remember, when you arrived and I said attendance is not mandatory here?"

"Yes," I nodded.

"We are able to offer students the flexibility of utilizing the technology you have just seen here remotely; in other words, virtual learning."

"So they can be anywhere?"

"Yes, but when they hit a rough spot, the digital or 'e-coach,' as we refer to it, will automatically send a file with the problem to a real teacher. When students return to class, the teacher is ready with the help the students need. Virtual learning cannot stand alone."

Students, teachers, classes—those words took on different meanings there. The line between student and teacher seemed blurred, and the term "class" could mean anything from a virtual journey through the vascular system to a mathematics tutorial on a hand-held electronic device. All of my sacred-cow definitions for "school" were being challenged.

"Is there anything in particular you would like to observe now?" Loren asked as she guided Barnabas and me through the "school."

Barnabas looked at me questioningly.

"Well," I thought. "It would be great to see how reading and writing are taught."

"Perfect, then let's go this way." And she redirected our path.

We entered a space that was a cross between a research and development lab and an art studio. Several activities were going on simultaneously in different areas. Some students sat around what looked like a still life; others were observing the movements of a small piece of equipment used to manufacture yoyos. In a sound-retardant area, a group of students watched what looked like two individuals debating, while the rest sat alone wearing headsets. Whatever they were doing, all the students used laptops.

"Can you guess at what is going on here?" asked Loren.

"You did say this was a reading and writing class, but I'm not certain what all the activities are."

Loren walked over to the students who were studying the still life.

"When you teach writing, do you teach different kinds of writing skills and styles?"

"Well, yes, I do," I replied.

"What are some of them?"

"There is descriptive writing and..."

"Well, students here are painting this still life with words. The writing program they are using is an e-coach that knows the still life they are trying to depict, and it is giving them hints as they write. At the end, they will have a score and a critique of their work. What other kinds of writing do you teach?"

"Persuasive, technical..."

Loren directed us to the group of students watching a debate and then to where students were observing manufacturing equipment.

"That is exactly what these two groups of students are learning."

"What about the students with headsets over there?" I asked. "What are they doing?"

"They are listening to music, testing their reading skills, and doing research. They also have the capability of converting text to voice and vice versa."

I shook my head in disbelief and thought about all the time I spent reading my students' essays and writing corrections, comments, and critiques.

"Does that mean the teachers don't read the essays?"

"Remember, real teachers cannot be replaced. They do read their students' essays along with the e-coach's corrections, critiques, and scores. The difference is that the e-coach can work with each student one-on-one, offering 'just-in-time' feedback—that is, at the time students most need to receive it. The e-coach also offers students completely objective and standardized evaluations of their work."

"You mean students never complain about favoritism or unfair grades from their e-coaches?" I smiled thinking of the many times students compared essays and scores.

"People will be people. But there is definitely less of that with this system. With much of the nuts-and-bolts corrections and comments done by the e-coach, the teacher has more time to help students with style, expression—some of the qualities and concepts that are best learned through human contact," Loren assured.

As Loren led the way out of the reading and writing area, one student's computer screen caught my eye; it looked like the student was editing a video.

"What is she doing?" I asked Loren.

"Oh, that's Leslie. She is working on her story-telling skills."

"But I thought this was a reading and writing class."

"It is. There are many multimedia-rich ways to tell stories. Digital video is not every student's choice, but for Leslie it is a way to demonstrate concepts learned and to exhibit academic achievement. We find this technology has the potential to inspire both students and educators to flex their imaginations."

After walking through several more learning areas, our host brought us to what looked like a "traditional" classroom. Students were seated at desks working with pencils. However, they also had those hand-held electronic devices I had seen in other areas of the school.

"What goes on here?" I asked. "A docudrama about schools of the past?"

"This is actually a math class," answered Loren, smiling politely at my irreverence.

And as we watched, I understood this was definitely no math class I had ever attended. The teacher was directing instruction from his laptop. The desks were actually touch screens on which the students could follow instruction, respond to questions, practice math skills, and be assessed. The pencils were styluses that students used to draw graphs and equations on their screens. Here again, Loren explained that the on-board e-coach provided just-in-time feedback to students.

"Loren, could you explain how the teacher in this class is being assisted to develop, select, and revise questions?" Barnabas requested.

"Sure, I'd love to talk about our 'classroom response system.' It allows the teacher to present a question or a problem and the students to then respond digitally. The system instantly compiles and summarizes students' answers for the instructor and for the students to see."

"How is that different from the e-coaches that not only evaluate student progress but also give them help along the way?" I asked.

"In some ways it is not different: it provides just-in-time feedback and it also provides individual student information to the teacher. But the 'classroom response system' is different in that it provides aggregated feedback to the teacher and the students. This can be used as the basis for large- and small-group discussions and problem-solving activities."

"I'm not sure I understand why the teacher or the learner would need aggregated feedback."

"Do you ever want to really understand your students' thinking processes and their opinions?"

"Yes, of course, and that is why we have class discussions."

"Do you believe that during those discussions you are getting all your students' opinions and ideas or even the ways in which they have thought through a given problem?"

I had to think about that for a moment. I remembered Luis and the rude awakening Barnabas had forced upon me. I thought back to the times when I had led class discussions. The truth is, there were a few students who always participated, some who participated some of the time, and a great many who did not participate at all.

"No, definitely not," I replied.

"Well, the teaching and learning communication tool I am using with this group of students fosters the sharing of ideas and opinions in a safe and anonymous environment. Responses can be displayed aggregately, like in a graph, for all to see and discuss. Students can learn from one another and the teacher can learn from the distribution of data."

"I think I understand. For example, I could ask a multiple-choice question that had more than one correct answer each and also one or more incorrect answers. After the students each replied, or voted, using this tool, I could display the distribution of the answers. Students could see how others answered compared to how they answered, and then a discussion could follow about how and why they answered as they did."

"Yes, that's a good example."

"That would be great 'just-in-time' feedback for me. If the entire class got a particular concept wrong, it would be clear to me that I had missed the mark."

"And it would be crystal clear to your students, too," Barnabas was quick to interject.

"Oops," I shuddered. "So true."

We all thanked the mathematics teacher for her time as she went back to her histograms and trend charts.

"What else would you like to see?" asked Loren, as she ushered us back through the mall-like schoolhouse.

"When we first entered, I saw some areas that looked a lot like the real-world—outdoor environments, labs, a medical center… "

"Yes, those are areas where students learn to apply what they have learned. We try to simulate the real world as best we can here; however, sometimes we have to resort to simulators."

"Simulators?" I questioned.

"Sorry, Loren, we'll have to take a rain-check on that," interrupted Barnabas as he looked at his watch.

I looked longingly back, thanking Loren and not wanting to ever leave. "I wish I could take all of this back with me."

"You can," said Barnabas.

"How?"

"In your understanding of what is possible."

"But even if this technology were invented, who would pay for it to be in my school or anyone's school?"

"Oh, the technology has been invented and it is available to you now. It is just a matter of time until folks come to understand the consequences of NOT providing ALL students and ALL teachers with these anywhere, anytime basic tools for learning. Tools with which students can control the speed they learn because the technology learns from them how to teach them, what to teach them, and at what speed."

"Basic tools, consequences—how is what we saw basic and what kind of consequences are you talking about?" I asked, quickly following Barnabas. "It sounds ominous."

"It is not just ominous: it is criminal. I want you to think of Luis again. What do you think is going to happen to him when he leaves school?"

"I'm not sure … without skills or anything," I replied, feeling full of guilt.

"Well, I'm not certain either, but, statistically, functionally illiterate people like Luis end up in some kind of trouble with the law and eventually in prison—70% in fact. That's criminal. So you pay now or you pay later for these basic tools—basic, because it is the most effective and efficient way of keeping the Promises of the Golden Pair to Luis and millions like him. Believe me, the price tag for Luis as an adult will be far greater than providing him and his teachers with the learning tools he needs now."

Barnabas' words hung heavily in the air as we drove through the quiet darkness. I'd never heard Barnabas this passionate, and all I could see was Luis, his head down, sitting in the back of the room, saying as little as possible and trying to make himself invisible. And the "Golden Pair." There was that term again. What had he meant by that? But just as I was about to ask, Barnabas broke the silence with, "Have you discovered the Fifth Promise, your promise to Luis?"

I forced myself to remember our conversation on the way to "the future." I focused on my wish to find just the right questions and in just the right time—beautiful questions for every subject, every concept, every skill, every fact, and tailored for every student.

"Yes," I finally declared. "It is to find the smallest possible piece of an idea, concept, or skill that can be tested with one simple question and answered with one simple answer. The result would leave the teacher in no doubt that the student understands. It is to promise to measure constantly."

"Exactly," confirmed Barnabas. *"I promise to constantly measure what you have learned from me."*

"But I can't make that promise, Barnabas, not in my drab, prehistoric classroom where my actions have criminal consequences! The reality of my situation is that I am stuck in the present. Why did you show me what is possible when it makes me even more frustrated about my limitations?"

Barnabas sighed deeply, "I'm sorry you feel that way," and then after a long pause, "Does that mean because Galileo did not have a nuclear telescope, he should not have attempted to study the stars? Or should Madame Currie have given up on discovering polonium and radium? The early explorers did not have compasses and other more precise navigational instruments, nor did they have big ships' engines. Should they have stayed home?"

I guessed those were rhetorical questions: no answers required. So we both sat in silence until the jeep stopped at the school.

As I sheepishly exited the vehicle, Barnabas remarked, "Invention is the most exciting and beautiful thing happening today; you can be a visionary in making it work for you or you can choose to ignore the possibilities." And he drove off.

My tired footsteps echoed in the desolate parking lot as I walked toward the school. The last place I wanted to see was my depressing classroom, but I needed my car keys; so, without turning on the lights, I groped around in my old desk drawer. There was, however, just enough light coming through the windows to illuminate the rows of student desks. The shadows drew images of students reading. In the half-light I saw Luis pretending to study. The memory of my trip to the "future" gave form to the drabness of the dark room; it lit my imagination with possibilities for "finding just the right questions and in just the right time—beautiful questions for every subject, every concept, every skill, every fact, and tailored for every student." Was that the Promise of the Golden Pair? Was that what I wished for and what my journeys with Barnabas had been all about? I repeated the Fifth Promise over and over again in my head. Finally, in the shadows of lost learning opportunities, I boldly added Promise Five to the other four. In my planner I circled Principle Five: *Learn fast!*

Promise # 1: I promise to teach YOU

Promise # 2: I promise to learn from YOU

how to teach YOU

Promise # 3: I promise to change my teaching based

on what YOU have taught me

Promise # 4: I promise to do my best to get YOU

to do your best

Promise # 5: I promise to constantly measure what

YOU have learned from me

That evening, I went home and researched every piece of technology that I had seen in the "future." Barnabas was right, they were all available, just not put to use in the way Loren had shown us. Some of the newest technologies, operational in the "classroom of the future," were still in their research and development stages and not really available to the public. The more I read, the more my imagination soared with the possibilities.

But how could I keep the Fifth Promise without the sophisticated tools I needed? What could I invent? What could I do to bring more of what I knew was needed to my students? I felt like I was starting from scratch so went back to my original four steps:

1. *Identify*—discover objectives that students need and want to learn
2. *Teach*—reach out to all students by being a performer, a communicator who gets and holds their attention
3. *Test*—watch, listen, formulate unique questions for each student by being an explorer, an adventurer
4. *Learn*—change how you teach by being an improviser, a creator

And then, if needed, do it all again and again by doing whatever it takes to achieve the learning objective

At which of the steps had I, and his other teachers, failed Luis? At a little of each, I guessed. We had not properly identified Luis' learning needs because we failed to learn from him how to teach him. Inversely, we could not learn from him how to teach him because we failed to properly identify his learning needs. Without clear learning objectives, most instruction, no matter how well delivered, is ineffective. As a result, Luis became an expert at skill/knowledge subterfuge. His other teachers and I definitely had not asked the right questions—beautiful questions in the smallest possible units—so that we could learn fast enough to teach him what he needed.

The next day, I approached my students as though each were Luis—with hidden skill and knowledge gaps. Making no assumptions about communication, I focused on steps three and four: *Test*, watch, listen, ask unique and *beautiful* questions; and *Learn* quickly how to change my teaching based on individual student feedback.

By the time I got to the last class of the day—Luis's class—my teaching had become veritably one-on-one with some small group instruction. I noticed that in order to be true to the Fifth Promise, I had to focus less on my teaching agenda and more on students' learning agendas. As I did that, the secrets of many Luises started to reveal themselves. Unlike Barnabas, I was no miracle worker; finding the gaps did not necessarily mean that I could mitigate the learning deficits overnight, or even over the course of that school year. However, what it did mean was that Luis and others could begin to take responsibility for their own learning. They discovered what they needed to know, what they needed to understand, and how they would be able to perform. It was my responsibility to ensure ways for them to practice in a safe environment so that failure did not scare them; on the contrary, all so-called setbacks were merely opportunities to do better the next time.

Luis, who was usually the first student out the door, lingered after class. When all the others had left, he was still working on a reading passage I had downloaded for him from an adult literacy site. The vocabulary and sentence structure were at a third-grade level, but the interest level was adult. It was not easy to find a good way to "test" and "learn" with Luis because he had such well-developed, clever methods of hiding. I tried to identify learning needs by testing covertly in as non-threatening a manner as possible. The adult literacy passage and associated activities I created for him comprised my first attempt at uncovering the secret. So, I was pleased when I saw, for the first time, that he was actually engaged in the class. I wondered why he hadn't left with the others.

"How's it going, Luis?"

He looked up at me and as though waiting for that cue asked, "Why did you give me this to read? It's not what the others got."

"Not everyone got the same assignments today," I replied.

"Some of my friends got the same ones and even got to work together."

"That may be, but I wanted you to try something different today. Is that okay?"

He did not answer.

Luis was a very large young man whose demeanor was incongruent with his stature. He moved slowly and rarely looked anyone in the eyes. He usually sat silent, slumped in his chair amidst a gaggle of smaller, animated guys who helped him academically as needed. He, in turn, "had their backs" for everything else.

"Did you finish? Would you like some help?"

Still no answer.

"It's really okay," I assured. "I can help and no one needs to know. We can work together before or after school. Once we go back to the very basics, your reading and writing will rapidly improve. There are some skills we'll need to work on together and then it will be up to you to build on them. Would you like to begin now?"

Luis approached my desk, pulled up a chair and sat across from me. His eyes never left the paper he was still holding. He set the incomplete page down on my desk between us, looked up and whispered hoarsely, "Can you teach me to read?"

"If you allow me, Luis. Only if you allow me." And that afternoon, Luis took the first steps toward teaching me how to teach him.

"People do not truly learn until they practice and fail in a safe environment."
Roger Shank

goldenpair

Chapter 6:

THE LAWS

The only kind of learning which significantly influences human behavior is self-discovered or self-appropriated learning, truth that has been assimilated in experience."

Carl Rogers

Over the next several weeks, I got better at "testing constantly for understanding," but I also got to thinking that all tests are not created equal and that some laws are easier to ignore than others. Take gravity, for example: that one is hard to overlook and easy to test. On the other hand, the laws of grammar, syntax, and literary style are easy to overlook and hard to test—hard because of their ambiguity. Gravity, on the other hand, is definitely black and white.

There is also the matter of importance. As a teacher of English, I found myself having to defend the relevance of everything I taught. I was struggling with connecting what the students were learning to how they could apply it in real life. While I was getting better at identifying learning needs, at teaching, testing, and learning, and re-teaching (ITTL), I had little confidence that the testing was of any consequence to the students. It was as if their learning took place in a vacuum. Even Luis, who had trusted me enough to teach me how to teach him, who was finally learning to read, believed that I could prepare him with skills he could apply to a career and higher education. I felt like I was letting him and all my students down because I was not providing real-world applications.

By that time, I felt certain Barnabas would show up with the Sixth Promise. He knew just the right time and just the right way. His student (me) was ready for the next lesson. In his absence, I examined ways I could make what I was teaching count for something in the lives of my students, but it all seemed so contrived. The classroom was not exactly the real world. I recalled the classroom of the future and the wonderful real-world labs I had seen. Loren had spoken about simulators, which I wished I had seen because then I might have been able to imagine more relevant approaches to the ITTL process.

Weeks went by but still no Barnabas. I was beginning to wonder if he was ever going to show up. Then on a crystal-clear, cool Saturday morning, a combination of impatience and frustration compelled me to drive to the airfield from which Barnabas and I had launched a number of our adventures. It seemed different that day—smaller and older. There was still the one building at the corner of the large field, but I had never noticed that it was in such disrepair. One solitary jeep was parked in the treeless parking lot. I parked next to the dusty vehicle and entered the building. A reception desk faced the door of a very small, empty waiting room.

"Hello!" I called, straining to see if anyone was around the corner behind the counter. "Barnabas, are you there?"

"Hi there. Can I help you?" came the reply from a woman walking briskly around the corner to greet me. "Oh! You must be the teacher, here for a lesson. Barnabas told us about you."

"About me? No, I don't think so … well maybe…" I stammered. "I'm not sure … what lesson … what do you mean?"

The woman had a kindly face, warm eyes, and a reassuring voice. "Barnabas made an appointment for you." She reached under the counter for a clipboard, turned a page and drew an imaginary line down a column of names. "Yes, here it is, right here."

I leaned over the counter and gasped at the sight of my full name, officially displayed on her roster titled: "Flight Instruction Schedule." How did it get there?

"There must be some mistake. I really didn't come for a flying lesson. You see, I don't fly."

"I know," said the woman, gently. "This is your first time," and she smiled in a way that reminded me of my doctor's expression the first time I had blood drawn.

"No, you don't understand. I don't fly and I don't want to learn to fly. I came here to find my … a … Barnabas…"

"Yes, I know that, too. He told us you would be coming for your lesson."

"He told … he … is he here?" I stammered, looking around.

"No, not yet. Actually, you are a bit early." She said, looking at her watch. "Can I get you a cup of coffee while you wait?"

"Isn't that his jeep?"

"Yes, it is. He is with another student right now—a beginner like you." And she gazed up at the sky. "Coffee?"

"Thanks, yes, please." The little waiting room was chilly and I needed something to warm me up. What had I gotten myself into this time? One thing was for sure: Barnabas was full of surprises. But how had he known that I would show up on that day and at that time?

"Here you are." The woman handed me the steaming coffee. "Cream and sugar are on the table," she added, pointing to a small, round table in the corner opposite the counter. I thanked her and wrapped my freezing hands around the warm cup. The comforting smell provided some normalcy to my situation and helped steady my nerves. As I turned toward the table to fix my coffee, a window revealed what looked like Barnabas' small plane coming in for a landing.

"Is that Barnabas?"

The woman glanced outside and confirmed, "It sure is and right on time, too." We both watched as Barnabas stepped out of the plane and onto the tarmac. However, I did not see a student with him.

"Where's the student?"

"Hmm … that's strange … I was sure he said he had a new student—a teacher like you."

"Well, well. So the mountain finally comes to Mohammed. It's about time!" Barnabas' large frame filled the doorway, his white hair lit like a halo by the outdoor light.

"You're right on time," he said and strode over to the counter to pick up the clipboard that kept the flight instruction roster. "Hey, Jenny. How's it going? That other student ever show up?"

"No, I thought he was with you."

"Well, now. You just never can be sure of some folks. They say they want to do something but then ... well ... it's just not their time."

"And you, New Teacher, is it your time—time to discover the Sixth Promise?"

"I thought you'd never ask."

"Come on, then. Let's get out of here before the afternoon wind starts to pick up, making it harder for you to handle her. So long, Jenny." Barnabas was out the door again before I could ask him what he meant by that.

"Have fun," Jenny called after him. "See you later."

I hurriedly thanked Jenny for the coffee and ran to catch up with Barnabas, who, by then, was back on the tarmac.

"Wait, wait, where are we going in such a hurry?" When I finally caught up with him, Barnabas was standing next to the plane he had just landed.

"The roster says you are here for a flight lesson. Your first."

"Barnabas, you know that's not the case. I came out here to find you because I've hit a brick wall again—with my teaching, I mean."

"What do you think is wrong?"

"That's what I came here to find out. It's like there is a disconnect between what I am teaching, the real world, and my testing ... it's, it's..."

"Irrelevant?"

"Yes, that's the word. It's irrelevant, and the classroom is such an artificial environment. Can we go back to the classroom of the future? I really want to see those simulators Loren spoke of. Maybe they will give me some ideas about how to make my *teaching more relevant and my testing more authentic.*"

"I could take you back there, but…" Barnabas hesitated and slowed his words down, "but I believe what I have in mind will help you much more."

There it was again—that doctor thing: you know it is going to hurt, but the person on the other end of the needle is trying to convince you that it is good for you.

"I'm totally not interested in learning to fly," I protested. "It's bad enough I get in this toy plane with you flying it. Trust me: you do not want me at the controls. I'm not even a very good driver!" With that, I started to walk away.

"Discovery learning!" Barnabas called after me.

"What?" I turned around.

"I said discovery learning—you know, one of those easy-to-ignore laws. That's how you will remember the Sixth Promise." I stood shaking my head in disbelief; he couldn't be serious.

"Come on, I'll show you. What's the worst that can happen? You may even enjoy it," he persisted.

"For once, Barnabas, can't you just TELL me the Sixth Promise?"

"Sure, but you won't learn it well enough to teach it," he insisted.

"There's got to be another way."

"Sure, there are an infinite number of ways, but this is the best way for you and me."

"Why?"

"Because I'm a pilot—a good one—and it's what I know best to help you discover what you need to learn about being a more effective teacher and learner."

As usual, Barnabas made good sense, but I was just not ready to get in that little airplane and sit behind the controls. My legs felt like tree trunks rooted to the ground as I looked from the aircraft to the endless runway and cloudless sky and then back to the aircraft.

"I can't do it Barnabas … I just can't do it. Can you give me a book or something … just to start?"

Barnabas broke into a fit of laughter. When he finally gained a modicum of control, tears running down his white skin, he managed to say:

"Oh, good, your passengers will be pleased to know you learned to fly 'by the book,'" and he fell back into uncontrollable laughter again. Noticing my expression of fear mixed with indignation, Barnabas regained his composure.

"Okay, I'll make a compromise with you."

A compromise—yes—I may get my cake and eat it too: learn the Sixth Promise and stay on the ground.

"What is it?" I asked.

Barnabas reached behind the pilot's seat of the plane and pulled out a manual.

"Here's the deal: you go home and learn the first two parts of this book, and I'll test you on your understanding tomorrow."

That's all I needed to hear: a 24-hour reprieve from impending terror. I grabbed the book and turned to leave before he changed his mind.

"What time and where?" I asked while heading for my car.

"Same time tomorrow. Right here."

"Okay," I shot back and raced to my car, clutching the big manual.

Dodging the proverbial bullet, I locked myself into my seatbelt and pulled quickly out of the airstrip parking lot, dust engulfing my car as I sped onto the road.

"Same time tomorrow. Right here." I replayed Barnabas' last words as I drove the familiar route back home. I had been in such a hurry to leave, I never asked him what kind of test it was going to be. As I waited at a red light, I looked at the manual that lay ominously, like a wizard's bible, on the passenger seat. The black leather cover was worn; the edges of the pages were yellowed and stained; the binding frayed like a well-used cook book. What if the first two sections were filled with impossible facts and figures I could not understand? What if I couldn't get through all five chapters? While I did not know much about flying, I guessed it involved science-related information like aerodynamics, physics, and other such subjects about which I knew very little. What if the test was actually flying the plane? A blaring horn called my attention to the green traffic light and back to driving. Once home, I settled into my favorite reading chair and cracked open the menacing *Student Pilot Flight Manual*. "Section One: Before the Fight; Section Two: Pre-Solo." It was going to be a long day.

By midnight, I had had about as much as I could stand of cockpit instruments and systems; aircraft parts and functions; definitions and the science of flight itself. It was tedious reading, with concepts probably much easier to understand had I had some hands-on opportunities. I wished then that I had not been so quick to leave what could have been the best manual of all: Barnabas and his little plane on the tarmac. So I closed my eyes and tried to picture the small craft, connecting it to the mind-numbing pages of the ancient manual. This was not discovery learning, I thought, as my eyelids shuttered the light.

"Alright, you can take the bike out, but it is way too big for you." Through heavy eyelids and the haze of half-sleep, I could see my mom in the kitchen of my childhood home. "It's in the basement. Make sure you dust it off before taking it out in public. Your brother hasn't used it for years."

"Thanks, mom." I was seven and chomping at the bit to ride my big brother's Schwinn two-wheeler.

"I wish you'd wait for your dad to get home. He could help, you know."

"I want to surprise him. I want him to see me riding on my own."

Mom shook her head, "Just come back in one piece. Stay on the sidewalk, and DON'T go off our block."

I wasn't sure I could get past our driveway, let alone the block. The bike was so beautiful: green and grown-up. I could see myself balancing perfectly for my dad when he got back from work. I'd make him proud and could honestly say I taught myself.

I dreamed of the many falls and recoveries; the bloody knees; the almost-balances, followed by more spills; and finally the pivotal point of "Yeah, I'm riding." The feeling was amazing: freedom of movement, a sense of abandonment, independence. I had wheels. I raced my dad home that evening, he on the road in his car, me on the sidewalk on my bike.

"I taught myself, dad! Aren't you proud?" But before he could answer, my beautiful dream was cut short by the thud of the *Flight Manual* crashing brick-like from my lap to the floor.

Ugh. I pulled myself out of the chair and back to the reality of what the next day would bring. If only I could feel about flying the same way I had felt about my bike. No fear, enthusiastic about the challenge, willing to practice and, most importantly, willing to make mistakes in order to learn. Learning was fun, and the test … well the test was performance. I wanted to surprise my dad by riding and I did: I passed the test. The price was a few bruises, cuts, and scrapes, but it was so worth it. Now, that was discovery learning, I thought, and dragged myself to bed.

After a few hours of deep, death-like sleep, I got ready to meet Barnabas. There was no way out if I wanted to learn the Sixth Promise, but there was also no way I'd be able to pass a test based on my understanding of the previous night's study. I could not remember a thing. None of it made sense. Yet I had a feeling that, in any case, the test would not be the objective of the day.

SOME LAWS ARE EASIER TO IGNORE THAN OTHERS

Manual in hand, I arrived at the airstrip on time and with Barnabas waiting in the same spot and position I had left him the previous day. As I approached, I could not help thinking about how much like an old photograph the scene resembled. It looked like a photo taken at an amusement park depicting you and your family or friends dressed up Western style in a saloon or at "Little House on the Prairie:" unbelievable, brownish-hued characters in implausible settings. I joined Barnabas on his sienna set—another dubious character.

"You're early," I greeted.

"Just wanted to catch up on some news before our ... I mean your test..." He unfolded and refolded the newspaper he'd been reading, framing the latest comic he wanted me to see.

"What do you think of this one?" and he gave me the well-read paper.

"It's a bit too à propos at this point to be funny. I had a really hard time with last night's assignment. I'm not ready for a test."

"Not even a paper-and pencil-type test?"

"Well, maybe, but what good would that do? I might be able to regurgitate some of the information that stuck in my head but I really don't understand the principles and purposes of what I read."

"Mm … let's see … why did you come out here yesterday? Something about 'making your teaching more relevant and testing more authentic,' wasn't it?" He took the manual from under my arm and opened it. "Attitude. What does the manual say about attitude?"

"It's one of the 'Big Three.' It was right at the beginning of the first section. I was able to get that on my own. The Big Three: Headwork, Air Discipline, and Attitude—the three essentials for the success of any pilot. Good Attitude to flying relates to how hard someone tries despite adversities."

"Good, that's right. What about the other kind of Attitude? The one that describes the plane?"

I shook my head, "No, I don't remember that." I had read something about the "Attitude" of aircraft but hadn't really understood the concept.

"Why do you think you were able to learn the first definition of 'Attitude' but not the second?"

"That's easy: I had a frame of reference for the first and no prior experience of the second. I mean, I probably could have memorized the meaning but, well, I just didn't have the patience or desire to do that. Besides, I was certain you wouldn't give me an, an …"

"An unauthentic test?" he coached.

"Yes," I thought for a moment. "I guess so."

The sun was rising quickly in the cool, blue morning sky, and the small plane began to sparkle in the banded blades of white light. I closed my eyes for a moment to recall some of the aircraft facts I had tried to learn the night before. When I opened my eyes, I felt a strange attraction to investigate first-hand what I had trouble fathoming during my torturous study session. Barnabas followed me to the plane and handed me a clipboard with a preflight inspection checklist.

"In God we trust", he said, "but everything else we check. Climb in."

I got into the cockpit while he looked on from outside the plane.

"Can you remember anything?" he asked as I looked at the rows of instruments. I shook my head.

"Here," he guided, "remove the control lock, turn on the master switch, and extend the flaps."

My hands moved hesitantly over the controls. "Then I need to check the landing light, anti-collision strobes, rotating beacon, and make sure the aircraft's master switch is off?" I asked, recalling a paragraph from the flight manual.

"That's right," Barnabas looked surprised at my recitation of text, but knew I was clueless about the application. He walked me through the process and then invited me to walk around the plane for the exterior preflight check. Clipboard in hand, I checked the control surfaces, antennas, landing gear, fuel level and fuel caps, oil, the works, in a systematic way that omitted nothing.

I became more comfortable realizing Barnabas' knowledge was beginning to pass from his head to my hands—knowledge that would eventually stick in my head as I learned to apply it.

Exterior preflight complete, Barnabas invited me back into the aircraft where I sat on the left, he on the right to show me the fire extinguisher, how to use my seat belt, and how to operate the doors. By the time we began the "engine start checklist," I was totally immersed in the excitement of real-world discovery learning, something I could not have done from the safety of my arm chair or the confusion of my book. Before I knew it, I was learning to taxi and, with Barnabas' help, I steered the airplane to the run-up area. Once again I performed additional preflight checks: flight controls, engine run-up, instruments, trim, and more.

"Time to take off."

I looked at Barnabas seated comfortably, hands on his set of controls, as if we were about to play a video game—one at which he'd beat his opponents a thousand times.

"Time to take off," I repeated in my mind: a rude awakening that we would soon leave the safety of the ground. The runway seemed to extend forever and it was, strangely enough, this "forever" that made me want to know what it felt like to fly on my own. Barnabas, his hands still safely on his set of controls, talked me smoothly through adding full power.

"Engine's good," he said and pointed to the airspeed indicator that had sprung to life.

I was so mesmerized by all that was happening around me, all so new, that Barnabas had to begin pulling the yoke back to achieve a "rotation" speed of 55 knots. When my head and hands started working again, I added my own pull; suddenly the ground dropped away and the runway disappeared beneath the nose of the plane. I was flying, and just as on that summer day I taught myself to ride a bike, I felt jubilant and free. Now this was discovery learning!

Climbing out, Barnabas suggested an airspeed of 75 knots, which was not a simple skill and certainly not like increasing the pressure on the gas pedal of your car. He showed me how to raise and lower the plane's nose to reduce and increase air speed. I pushed and pulled, but it didn't make sense.

"Now, you are learning about the other kind of aircraft Attitude."

"But I'm still not getting it."

"You never operated in three dimensions before. Be patient." Barnabas, still completely composed and in video-game demeanor, used his own controls to pin the airspeed needle on 75 knots. By then, I was on stimulus overload, bombarded with new sounds, sights, and sensations. I could hardly concentrate on Barnabas' instructions on how to level off and trim the airplane for straight and level flight.

"Watch!" he pointed out. "See how the craft tends to fly straight and level on its own." The less he controlled it, the better we flew.

At the risk of trying to do two things at once, I said, "Not unlike learning to ride a bike: the more you try to adjust, the more likely you are to fall; whereas, if you just maintain forward movement, you are more apt to stay vertical."

"Good analogy, watch again," and he gently banked us about 30 degrees. "Follow along with me on your controls," he encouraged as we did another. We repeated this several times together until I realized Barnabas was allowing me to bank on my own. He offered some suggestions and encouragement, but was mostly silent allowing me to learn in my own— more ITTL and discovery learning.

"Time to head back."

Back … back was the airport, and for the first time since we took off, I was keenly aware of our distance from the ground and the safety of the airstrip. I had no idea where we were. Feelings of agoraphobia mixed with vertigo led me to gladly surrender control of the craft to Barnabas, whose experienced eyes easily picked out where we needed to go.

Landing called for another checklist and a descent. Barnabas knew I was overwhelmed so simply asked me to take note of what he did to reduce power and maintain vigilance for other air traffic. He explained the basics of traffic patterns and something about being downwind, parallel to the runway on the left. He made adjustments to the flaps, made a left descending turn he called a base leg and reduced the power again. Another left turn put us on final approach. A moment later, the ground rushed up, the airplane's nose rose and I felt a gentle bump. Hello, Mother Earth. After more off-runway check-lists—all done seemingly by long-established rite and ritual—we headed back to the parking lot.

While Barnabas and I had had some serious adventures discovering the Promises of the Golden Pair, they paled in comparison to the quest for the Sixth Promise. There may not have been time-travel, nor high-tech schools of the future, nor high-sea dramas, but my lesson with Barnabas, during which I discovered the elements of flight and flying, pushed the corners of my comfort zone.

"Want a cuppa?" Barnabas asked as he headed toward the little building that served as a terminal.

"I could use a warm brew to settle my nerves," I answered.

"Jenny usually makes a fresh pot around now; lots of folks drop in this time of day."

"Lots of folks?" I asked tongue in cheek.

"Yup, this is when they show up."

Barnabas was right about one thing: the smell of freshly brewed coffee filled the little waiting area with a delightful aroma.

"Where's Jenny?" I asked and looked around the empty room. There were old photos of small planes hanging cattywonkus; a large corkboard displaying yellowed charts and checklists; and clipboards dangling from hooks, all randomly assigned to olive-green walls. However, there did not seem to be a rush of "folks" for the java—not even Jenny.

"I expect she's in the back keeping all our paperwork straight. It's a hard job, you know, staying in good stead with the FAA. She's an angel."

"Like you?"

"Uh … well … I don't know about that one."

He poured us both coffees and sat down in one of the decidedly uncomfortable plastic green chairs. The chair creaked as he leaned back, slung his right ankle over his left knee and took a long luxurious sip of black coffee. I fumbled with cream and sugar at the table under the waiting room's one window that offered a clear view of the runway.

"Here's where we would have a post-flight debrief if you were going to go up again, and we'd talk about the laws that are impossible to ignore like …"

"… gravity and Bernoulli's Principle … inertia and …"

"Alright! You did learn a thing or two from the manual."

"And from high-school physics classes, but the laws were never as real to me as they were in the air this morning."

"Excellent, but since you are here to learn more about *the laws that are easy to ignore,* let's debrief on those."

"You mean like the Law of Discovery Learning."

"Yes, and the Law of Primacy."

"What's that?"

"What you learn first you remember first: first in, first out. Those two easy-to-ignore laws are intrinsically connected and specific to what you came here to learn today. Remember what you said you wanted to know, understand, and be able to do?"

I walked over to the chair next to him and pulled it forward from the wall so I could face him as we talked.

"Yes, and it wasn't flying," I teased. "I want to learn how to make my *teaching more relevant and my testing more authentic.*" I stirred my coffee and thought about how frustrated I was in unsuccessfully trying to make my instruction count for something in the lives of my students; it all seemed so contrived because the classroom was not exactly the real world.

"You did a good job up there," Barnabas interrupted my thoughts, "and after all that fuss, I believe you actually had a good time."

"I have to admit it was something I would never have tried on my own. But it really gave me a new perspective."

"How so?"

"First of all, I've never had to be so precise about anything: checklist after check-list, and so many redundancies for safety. The fact I had to operate in three dimensions at all times was in itself an eye-opener. Working past a few adrenalin rushes reminded me of diving, but gave me the advantage of an unlimited supply of air, so I could actually bring my breathing back under control after a few hints of hyper-ventilation. It made me feel more competent ... more confident."

"Like when you taught yourself to ride a bike?"

"Yes, exactly..." I ceased being amazed by how much this man knew about me.

"Anything else?"

"The Law of Discovery Learning—one of those easy-to-ignore laws—does not necessarily mean teaching yourself."

Barnabas swirled the black coffee around in the white Styrofoam cup and waited for me to continue.

"I think discovery learning means being placed in a real-world environment in which you can experience and learn while being guided. Like the way we practiced banking and flying straight and level."

"Do you think Discovery Learning ever involves solo learning?"

"Probably, like when I taught myself to ride my bicycle. The problem was I paid a pretty high price for that skill. Had I waited for my dad to help me, I may not have had so many spills, bruises, scrapes, and tough-to-break bad habits. While that worked for a seven-year old riding a bike, I wouldn't want to teach myself to fly."

"Yeah, sounds like it would be another high-stakes, killer test." Barnabas teased, referencing my frightening SCUBA experience with Larry the wind-up dive instructor. "But even if you could teach yourself to fly, which the very first aviators managed to do, the thing to remember is your teacher will only be as skilled as you."

I thought about the many teaching and learning experiences I had had with Barnabas over the past few months; his experience and skills provided a model and gave me the confidence to break out of my comfort zones. The thought of being relegated to a teacher no better than I was a dismal thought.

"Who's that?" I jumped as I heard the familiar roar of a small plane on the runway. I strained to see through the dusty window.

"Another of my students," he answered without looking. "Touch and goes. She's practicing take-off and landing and is almost ready to go solo. Any other insights?" he pressed.

I thought for a moment, listening to the muffled engine intervals. "I am surprised by how something as scary as learning to fly and as obscure as studying a flight manual could turn-out to be so wonderfully alive in less than an hour. I will never forget what I learned today. Never!"

"Do you know why?"

"It was new and exciting and it captured my senses."

"And it involved the other easy-to-ignore law: the *Law of Primacy*."

"What you learn first you remember first: first in, first out," I repeated Barnabas' definition.

"Yes, that is why it was important for you to have a good, first-time teaching and learning experience in the air. Anything less would have put you at risk for learning incorrect information and skills. The Law of Primacy dictates that, right or wrong, you will remember best what you learned first. In tandem, the longer you hold false ideas or incorrect skills, the harder they are to fix, no matter how many times you are exposed to correct information and skill training."

"I suppose then, based on the Law of Primacy, the newest students should have the oldest teachers."

"By oldest I take it you mean the most experienced, best teachers."

"Yes ... sorry ... I didn't mean to imply..."

"That would be optimum," Barnabas agreed. "It's a shame it rarely happens."

Barnabas thought for a moment while fiddling with the laces on his boat shoes.

"So how did your experiences with the laws—hard-to-ignore and easy-to-ignore—relate to teaching relevance and testing authenticity?"

Trying to connect the dots, I hesitantly began, "When presented with the opportunity for experiential—discovery—learning, I became more engaged. Without a teacher or coach, the flight manual made little sense and I really wasn't motivated to teach myself. I had no frame of reference and I simply was not interested; however, when I got to the airport this morning, my desire to acquire the knowledge and skills I had not been able to master last night was ignited by a real-world, relevant, learning environment. My very life depended on me understanding the hard-to-ignore laws related to the science of flying. It was through the act of discovery (the Law of Discovery Learning) that I became *motivated*, and it was through the carefully, expertly guided, first-time flying experience (Law of Primacy) that I will always remember today's lesson of flying fundamentals."

Barnabas traced the rim of his cup with his index finger. "So you feel certain learning took place?"

"Absolutely!"

"What makes you so certain?"

"I was continuously tested, and results were delivered immediately by you and the aircraft, providing me with a rudimentary but realistic assessment of my flying knowledge and skills."

"Then what does that say about the authenticity of the testing?"

"It was totally authentic and immediately connected to learning objectives that were very relevant. It's pretty obvious, as you pointed out yesterday, that no one is going to learn to do what we did up there today by reading a manual and then taking a paper-and-pencil test." I stopped to reflect on the way in which Barnabas structured my flight lesson. He believed I could learn and figured out how to engage me; he identified my learning needs; he learned from me how to teach me, providing continuous feedback and changing his teaching to accommodate my learning. Even though the learning environment was dynamic, he did his best to get me to do my best. I learned fast and because I knew nothing, he started me at the most fundamental level. He kept the first Five Promises ... but what about the Sixth?

"So what if today's lesson was an example of relevant teaching and authentic testing, Barnabas? The classroom simply does not provide the same kinds of opportunities for real-world learning and authentic assessment in an environment like ... like the experience I just had ... without the help of ... well ... simulators or something."

"Last time I looked, you didn't have simulators in your classroom." He placed both feet on the grounds and leaned forward towards me. "Why do you need them?"

"To help students connect what they are learning to the real world."

"If your teaching objectives are in line with the students' learning objectives and if the students' learning objectives are in line with what they need and want to know, understand, and do, then how can there be a question about relevance?" He leaned even closer to me and I could see the orange flecks in his hazel eyes. His brow furrowed beneath tussled white hair. Despite myself, I pushed my chair back slightly to avoid the unsettling penetration of Barnabas' gaze. I sat up a little taller and watched the student pilot continue to practice touch and goes.

"So, you are saying that relevance begins with the learning objectives, no matter what the subject, even English."

"Of course," he exclaimed, slapping his knee with one hand and spilling coffee with the other. "Why would you teach something that a student will never use in the 'real world'? If you and your student can't define the relevance of a learning objective, why teach it?"

"Just like I couldn't find a reason to learn the stuff in the flight manual?"

"That's right: it wasn't relevant to you at the time and you had no frame of reference for the information."

"But it began to make sense to me during the hands-on lesson that included … oh, I get it … that included the testing! *You test the learning close to the way that it will be used in the future.* That way it will be authentic."

"Yes, and if you choose your test wisely, *it should prove the learning objective with efficiency and beauty.*"

"How would I know that?"

"Easy. Here's the litmus test: if the test requires students to provide authentic answers, then it is itself authentic. Example: Do you agree flying is a skill that is done in the real world?"

"Of course."

"But I gave you a manual to read when you refused to fly yesterday."

"Yes."

"When you got here this morning, you did not know how you would be tested; but you did know you were unprepared."

"Right again."

"Had I given you a paper-and-pencil test—perhaps even multiple-guess— would that have been authentic?"

"Well … no …"

"Why not?"

"Because all it would have proved was that I could memorize stuff from a book. It would not have told you anything about my ability to do that…" and I pointed to the window where the student pilot had just made her final landing.

"Was there testing that went on during our lesson today?"

"Yeah, tons."

"Give me an example of one."

"Banking: we practiced banking together, and when you thought I was ready, you let me take the controls on my own."

"It was an efficient and beautiful way to find out authentically if you could bank a plane. So, you see, first make certain your objectives are relevant and then wisely choose a test to prove the learning objectives have been met. And that brings us to the Sixth Promise, which I believe you know by now."

"Remember that what my students learn from me will be used by them in the real world?"

"Yup, that's it."

I left the airport that morning with the sun high in the sky and a new personal challenge on the horizon: make everything I teach relevant. Every learning objective had to have the potential for real-world application. Only then could testing be authentic.

goldenpair

Conclusion:

THE GOLDEN PAIR

"Founding itself upon love, humility, and faith; dialogue becomes a horizontal relationship of which mutual trust between the dialoguers is the logical consequence."
Paulo Freire

Barnabas walked me to my car and watched as I drove off. Just as his image would be indelibly fixed in my rear view mirror, so would his teaching be in my mind.

"Keep smiling, New Teacher! Practice love and keep making a difference!" he called after me. I knew somehow that would be the last time I saw him, No need for good-byes. He had fulfilled his mission, a mission that began with a promise to take me back to the fundamentals of learning and teaching; fundamentals he said I knew, but had forgotten; fundamentals I would need if I was serious about making a difference. He made a Promise: Six Promises to help me fulfill my desire for an excellent learning and teaching environment.

"My motives are simple," he had confessed. "Pure and simple." Pure, simple, and filled with love. During that first strange encounter, Barnabas explained it was his job to know when someone needed and wanted help. He came to "work miracles" because he knew I was ready: I cared enough about my students to want to make a difference in their lives.

The day was still so beautiful, I couldn't bear the thought of going indoors, even though I had my work cut out for me defining relevance in my students' learning objectives. On the way back home, I took a detour through the neighborhood where I had grown up. It hadn't changed much from the day my mother first walked me to school and left me with strangers. The houses looked smaller and older; my school was the same except for having been renamed after one of its principals—ironically, the same principal with whom my mom had disagreed vehemently about my third-grade placement. I slowed down to take a better look at the new, conspicuously contemporary name plaque. What an eyesore!

I parked on the street that I had looked out on from my bedroom window and walked along its tree-lined sidewalk. There was a quiet buzz of children playing in the park across the street. Dogs led their owners around benches and tugged toward tolerant trees waiting to be watered. I found a solitary bench and sat down to look at the places where I had lived, learned, played, and matured; where my mother would call me to come back home; where I learned to play with others; and where, I thought, the seeds of the Golden Pair may have been first planted. The Golden Pair, the Golden Pair … what was it? What did those two words mean? How is it that in all this time, I had not thought about them? I had been so intent on establishing the Promises, that I had forgotten to ask about the significance of the "Golden Pair."

A young child was playing close to his mother with a push toy, one that played music as it rolled along—music hard to get out of your head. The mom was showing the child how to push the toy so that the whirly thing-a-ma-bob went round and round playing the simple tune. He was delighted with the results, clapped his hands begging for "more, more!" The mom placed the toy in her small son's hands and encouraged him to try. At first, the boy was not able to push it well enough to achieve the same contiguous motion and music as his mother had. So mom showed him again and again in different ways; then they did it together; and finally, he was able to do it several times on his own, much to his gleeful satisfaction. Sometimes he would run the toy up to a rock or get it caught in a crack in the sidewalk. At those times, his mother would guide him around the barrier until together they found a way around it. I noticed how the toy and its music took the boy away from his mother; at first he ventured a short way and after a silent exchange of facial expressions and body language between him and his mother, he quickly returned. As the boy trusted his mother would not leave him and the mother trusted the boy could and would return, the noisy roundtrips between mom and the world got longer and longer until boy and mom were comfortable with being an eye or ear shot away. There was an unspoken communication—connection—by which he was learning about his toy, the environment, and about how far he could safely venture.

As I watched, I was reminded of the instruction I had received from Barnabas just a few hours earlier in the sky. There was no difference between the beautiful teaching and learning dialogue that went on between mother, son and whirly, noisy push toy and that which went on between Barnabas, me and the whirly, noisy airplane. To the mother and son, the challenges were, relatively speaking, equally great and the stakes equally high. Underlying both scenarios were the Six Promises and—and, I realized—the Golden Pair!

There it was all the time: Each time the Six Promises are fulfilled, the teacher and learner create a Golden Pair. The mom and her son were a Golden Pair just as Barnabas and I had become a Golden Pair. Each one of my students and I had the potential to become a Golden Pair—if I fulfilled each of the Six Promises. The Secret was right under my nose the whole time Barnabas was helping me discover the simple fundamentals of teaching and learning. I then understood that the Golden Pair was an educational idea that looked at the teacher and the student as a Pair whose relationship was, in its ideal manifestation, "Golden."

I continued to watch mother and son as they lovingly danced the beautiful dance of dialogue, of teaching and learning, of the Golden Pair. I thought of my own mother and how thoroughly she kept the Six Promises. From my first Golden Book to my last great push for independence, ours was a grand dialectic dance—a Golden Pair. How had I forgotten all that, so simple, so right?

When I returned to my classroom the next day, I added the Sixth Promise to the others and circled Principle Six, in my planner: *Some laws are easier to ignore than others!*

Promise # 1: I promise to teach YOU

Promise # 2: I promise to learn from YOU

how to teach YOU

Promise # 3: I promise to change my teaching

based on what YOU have taught me

Promise # 4: I promise to do my best to get YOU

to do your best

Promise # 5: I promise to constantly measure

what YOU have learned from me

Promise # 6: I promise to remember that what YOU

learn from me will be used by YOU in the real world

It wasn't as difficult as I thought it would be to connect the students' learning objectives to real-world scenarios. Where I had gaps, I would ask the students to help. If we were unable to define the relevance of a learning objective, the students and I would rethink the objective that might just need to be revised or reframed. For example, Lily had a keen interest in fashion design: she continuously drew in class, everything from "gotta-have" accessories to runway models displaying her newest line of skimpy swimsuits. Her writing assignments were usually adorned with some or all of these designs. But whereas the designs were gifted and meticulously crafted, the writing was not. Lily had the potential to write well; we just had not made the connection between writing and her passion for fashion design. Therefore, we had to reexamine her learning objectives as they pertained to writing; we needed to understand how they connected to HER real world—her reverie. In Barnabas' words: "Why would you teach something a student will never use in the 'real world'? If you can't define the relevance of a learning objective to the student, why teach it?" Even if Lily's passion for fashion design changed over the years, it was real to her at that time in her learning, and I had to take advantage of that teachable moment.

The first day of the Sixth Promise went well and I was anxious to go home and decompress before reviewing the day's work. As had become routine at the end of each day, I circled the tables and chairs picking up papers and other debris that had been left in adolescent haste. When I came to the seat Barnabas had occupied the day of our first unbelievable meeting, I stopped. Nearly three months had gone by since he had mysteriously appeared in my classroom. It was time void of chronology, in which he had taken me from frenetic to fascinated; haughty to humble; and teacher to learner. Even the classroom had been transformed, perhaps not physically, but it had evolved into a place where the idea of the Golden Pair could become a reality as each student and I formed a one-on-one Pair that was Golden. It indeed had the ingredients of an excellent learning and teaching environment. Thank you, Barnabas!

With the last of my ritual clean-ups complete, I packed the books and papers I would take home.

"Excuse me," came a small voice from outside the door. "Excuse me but do you have any extra copies of *Jonathan Livingston Seagull*. I don't seem to be able to find enough for a class set and, well, you know what happens when you ask students to share." A young woman poked her head in the door and stood meekly between me and … the end of my day! Unsure of the right way to act, she hastily added, "I'm having … well … the administration thinks that … I have problems with classroom management. You know … discipline and all that."

"Hi, aren't you Mr. Adams' replacement for the term?" I put my books down.

"Yes, I'm Liza, short for Elizabeth. I just started last week. It's a terrible thing," she paused, "about his wife, I mean. I hope she gets better."

I nodded. "How's it going? Did he leave you lesson plans and learning objectives—a syllabus?"

"No not really," she replied hesitatingly, and I recognized her startled look all too well. "I haven't been able to find much of what he was planning, but the students said they were reading *Jonathan Livingston Seagull,* so I thought it would be good for them to finish it. Do you have any?"

My thoughts drifted back to the first day I met Barnabas and how much like me Liz seemed to be.

"Any books," she clarified as my attention drifted from *Jonathan* to Barnabas.

"Oh, books, yes … I'm sorry … let me check." I walked to the bookshelves at the back of the room and pulled out a few dusty copies of the paperback.

"Thanks, I really appreciate it," she said as I handed her the precious bounty that she believed would help her "classroom management."

"Sorry to bother you while you're trying to leave for the day. You're a life-saver," and she turned to go.

"That's okay. Let me know if there's anything else you need."

Liz turned around, studied my face for a moment, and then, as if she recognized a possible lifeline, beseeched, "I'm not sure how I'm going to get through this semester. I just don't feel prepared. I really want to encourage my students, but nothing seems to work. Can you help?"

Liz's last question made me recall one of the first things Barnabas ever said to me: "It's my job to know when someone wants help. Everyone has a miracle-worker, but they don't realize it until they accept the fact that they need one. Most people don't believe they need help, so they don't get it. The other part of my job is to know when someone cares enough about a fellow human that they want to make a difference in their lives; that tells me they are ready for a miracle. That's when I show up." Well I was no Barnabas but I certainly wanted to help.

"Yes," I encouraged, "but, we'll need to go back to the fundamentals of learning and teaching—fundamentals you know, but have forgotten—fundamentals you'll need if you are serious about making a difference."

"That would be amazing," she gushed then stopped to notice the Six Promises written on the whiteboard. "What are those?" she asked.

"A means to the Golden Pair: the tools you'll need for the job you want to do."

"I don't understand."

"You will."

"When can we start?"

"Tomorrow?"

"Sure thing. Will it take long?"

I smiled thinking about her question in relation to my own impatient journey and remembered Barnabas' warning that "There are no magic bullets to your 'perfect teaching and learning environment,' and while you can wish for the power of a Vulcan 'mind-meld,' you'll have to ask yourself if that is really teaching"

"That's up to you. There are no magic bullets," I answered, "no guarantees of success—just a promise to never stop trying and always keep learning."

"Okay" she responded dubiously and we agreed to meet the following after-noon for our first adventure.

"Oh, one other thing, I called after her as she turned to leave, "it's a line in *Jonathan*. Think of it as your first assignment."

"Yes…?"

"Keep working on love."

A disciple is not above his teacher, but everyone who is perfectly trained will be like his teacher. Luke6:40

goldenpair

Epilogue:

KEEPING THE SIX PROMISES OF THE GOLDEN PAIR

"The teacher who walks in the shadow of the temple, among his followers, gives not of his wisdom but rather of his faith and lovingness."

Kahlil Gibran

Although I grew up in the city, my family and I used to spend our summers at the beach. One of my favorite things to do at the beach was fly kites with my dad. These were not your ordinary kites that could be purchased at a store. These were kites designed and built by my dad and me. So really, half the fun of flying kites was making them. Each year we would make the best kite: one that was better than the year before. It would fly higher, last longer, and had the most beautiful designs. One day I learned an important lesson about kite-flying: no matter how great your kite may seem, there is always an essential element which is out of your control—the wind.

My dad was a very detail-oriented person, so these creations could take several weeks to design and build. My anticipation grew with each day as I looked forward to the moment we could fly it. Sundays were my dad's days off and he promised that the very next Sunday we would fly our kite. He promised and I was so excited. That Sunday I gobbled my breakfast in anticipation of flying the biggest most beautiful kite I had ever seen. When we got down to the beach my dad warned that the kite might not fly because there was not enough wind.

"But you promised," I cried with disappointment. "You promised!"

My dad was definitely a man of his word and took the word "promise" very seriously; but as he had warned, the biggest, most beautiful kite of all would not take off the ground. Now had it been any other dad, I think he would have given up, lectured me on how there are just some things that are too difficult or out of our control and call it quits. But not my dad, he took a look at that kite, looked up at the sky and said:

"Yes I promised, but we are going to have to redesign the kite to fly in really low wind conditions. It is not going to look like it does now. Is that okay with you?"

"Okay, certainly it is okay. I just want the kite to fly. But what are you going to do?"

"I'm not sure yet, but we'll figure it out together. So my dad and I kept redesigning that kite until it wasn't the biggest or the most beautiful kite anymore, but it was certainly the best—the best because it could fly under just about any wind conditions. We flew the kite that day. My dad did whatever it took to keep his promise.

It may not be today or tomorrow, but some day, the students you teach, the children you raise, the people with whom you communicate will know that you have done everything in your power to keep the Six most basic Principles and Promises that underlie all teaching and learning situations. And as they pass these on to those they teach, tutor, counsel, coach, nurture, they, too, will understand the secret of the Golden Pair—an educational idea that looks at the teacher and the student as a pair and when the pieces of this idea fall into place, it is Golden.

goldenpair

Dr. Alexandra Penn was born and raised in New York City. She attended Hunter College of the City University of New York for both her undergraduate and graduate work. Her classroom and administrative experiences include 25 years of working with children, youth and college students; her consulting work in curriculum and staff development has taken her across the United States and abroad. Penn is the author of several professional articles and books and the creator of the first Aerospace Career Academy in Florida. She is a former Governor-appointed trustee to Brevard Community College; visiting professor at the University of South Florida; and special advisor to the Florida Commissioner of Education. Alex, as she prefers to be called, is a tried-and-true school reformist and Senior Consultant for GoldenPair & Company, a Florida-based school-choice consulting organization.

24107385R00080

Made in the USA
Charleston, SC
12 November 2013